BEASTLY BEHAVIOUR

BEASTLY BEHAVIOUR

More True Animal Tales

by Rolf Harris

Mark Leigh & Mike Lepine

Illustrations by Rolf Harris

Century · London

First published by Century in 1997

1 3 5 7 9 10 8 6 4 2

Copyright © Rolf Harris and Iliterati International Ltd 1997

Illustrations © Rolf Harris 1997

Rolf Harris, Mark Leigh and Mike Lepine have asserted their
right under the Copyright, Designs and Patents Act, 1988 to
be identified as the authors of this work

First published in the United Kingdom in 1996 by Century
Random House, 20 Vauxhall Bridge Road,
London SW1V 2SA

Random House Australia (Pty) Ltd
20 Alfred Street, Milsons Point, Sydney,
New South Wales 2061, Australia

Random House New Zealand Limited
18 Poland Road, Glenfield, Auckland 10, New Zealand

Random House South Africa (Pty) Limited
Endulini, 5a Jubilee Road, Parktown 2193, South Africa

Random House UK Limited Reg. No. 954009

A CIP catalogue record for this book is
available from the British Library

Papers used by Random House UK are natural, recyclable
products made from wood grown in sustainable forests. The
manufacturing processes conform to the environmental
regulations of the country of origin.

ISBN 0 7126 7819 0

Design and make-up by Roger Walker
Set in 12/16pt Adobe Minion

Printed and bound in Great Britain by
Mackays of Chatham, plc, Chatham, Kent

Contents

ACKNOWLEDGEMENTS

The authors would like to thank the following people for their invaluable help and assistance:

Helena Firth-Powell, Margy Frost, Julie Hall, Louise Hartley-Davies, Andrea Hatton, Mary and Dennis Hatton, Kathleen Holland, Beth Humphries, Gill and Neville Landau, Debbie Leigh, Edith and Philip Leigh, Eileen and Harold Lepine, Philippa Hatton-Lepine, Judy Martin, Tony Peake, Liz Rowlinson and Shirley and David Thomson.

Chapter One
AGAINST THE ODDS

To Zan the badger, it was just what she was looking for –
a snug and warm ready-made badger's set. All she had to
do was climb in, curl up and have 40 winks. Unfortunately for
Zan, what she thought was a set was actually a Zanussi washing
machine. Snuggled deep down under all the dirty clothes, she
was completely invisible to the machine's owner, Min Muldoon
of Petersfield. Min switched on the machine – and Zan got a
rude awakening, squirted with warm soapy water and spun
around and around and around. It wasn't until Min unloaded
the machine that she discovered Zan, dazed and fluffy, but
otherwise almost completely unharmed!

Zan – who was named after the washing machine she was
found in – was packed off to convalesce at the Hydestile Wildlife
Sanctuary in Surrey, where, despite her experience, she soon
settled back into her favourite pastime – finding a snug, dark
place and curling up for a nap!

When Cindy the Jack Russell became trapped down a
disused mine shaft, police officers and the fire brigade
joined forces with the RSPCA to try to rescue her. They put their
own lives at considerable risk, trying to gain access to the
furthest reaches of the crumbling mining tunnels, where they
could hear Cindy whining for help, while her distraught owners
waited at the entrance. They battled on for days, but there

seemed to be no way to get at the helpless little dog, whose cries were getting ever more weak and pitiful. In the end, the authorities held a meeting and decided that, rather than letting Cindy face a slow death of starvation alone in the dark, the only humane thing to do would be to collapse the mine with dynamite. Experts were brought in, the old mine tunnels wired up and then destroyed in a huge explosion.

Cindy's owners returned home heartbroken. Several hours later, as they were still consoling each other, Cindy turned up at the door, grubby and thin but unhurt. The explosion had torn away most of the rock trapping her and she was then able to scramble her way to freedom . . .

Should he pull the red wire, or should he pull the blue wire? The little stray mongrel who had just sniffed out a semtex bomb in a shop doorway in Domazlice, in the Czech Republic, didn't know. So he took a wild gamble – and relieved himself all over the bomb! Strangely this technique – not one approved by highly trained army disposal experts – worked and the bomb failed to explode.

When a huge wave knocked golden retriever Coconut Harry overboard off a yacht in the Florida Keys last year he proved himself a true sea dog – and set a possible world record for the doggy paddle! Harry had put to sea with his mistress, Naomi Simonelli, and her boyfriend, to celebrate Naomi's birthday. At first the weather looked fine, but then a sudden storm overtook their boat and, just as Harry was scampering forward to the bow, a powerful wave smashed against them pitching him into the sea. Naomi raised the alarm and soon a small flotilla of coastguard cutters and private yachts were out scouring the ocean for the dog, but as darkness fell there was still no sign of the four-year-old retriever.

Naomi refused to give up hope. She had hundreds of leaflets printed with pictures of Harry on them, and posted them to all the beachfront homes. She went on the radio to appeal for people to keep a lookout, and all the local papers featured big pictures of Harry but still there was nothing. It looked like Coconut Harry had gone . . . there was no news from anywhere.

Until eight days later that is, when a group of research scientists made a trip to tiny Monkey Island – a desolate and otherwise uninhabited isle in the Keys, which is home to 1,000 rhesus monkeys. Upon arrival, the scientists were baffled. The monkeys were clearly traumatised by something. They kept leaping about the treetops, screeching and yelling. The reason soon became apparent – a big, shaggy, smelly, golden retriever was sunning himself right in the middle of their territory. After being knocked overboard, Harry had doggy-paddled through stormy, shark-infested waters for more than five miles, before dragging himself ashore on Monkey Island!

Reunited with his owner, Harry soon recovered. 'It's a miracle he survived,' says Naomi. 'When I got him home he was looking very thin and tired and has lost about 10lbs – but he still managed to wag his tail when he saw me.

'As soon as he was up and about again, the first thing he did was to jump straight into the canal at the bottom of my garden!'

Harry clearly hasn't been put off water by his extraordinary adventure – but Naomi says that the next time she takes him out she's going to make sure that Harry's wearing a life jacket . . .

'Like a modern-day Toto' was how Sadie, a Yorkshire terrier, was described in 1993, after being sucked up by a tornado as she played in the garden of her owners, James and Sandra Davis of Saginaw, Texas. But unlike the little dog in *The Wizard of Oz*, Sadie didn't have a gentle landing in Munchkinland. She was whipped into the sky by the powerful twister, according to a neighbour who saw her swept upwards as he was running for cover.

Fortunately, the Davis family were out when the tornado struck, but they returned home to find their house devastated. They searched the surrounding countryside for their little dog, following the path the tornado had taken – evident by the wreckage it had left behind on its trail of destruction. There was no sign of Sadie and the family returned, convinced they had lost both their home and their beloved pet.

They'd given up hope of ever seeing her again, when out of the blue, a couple of days later, they got a call from someone who'd found their dog two miles away, still wearing her collar and name tag.

The Davises drove there as fast as they could. Sadie was alive and well – and apart from a few minor bruises, none the worse for her aerial journey.

A single flock of North American passenger pigeons observed in 1810 contained roughly two billion birds! Unbelievably, by 1914, the whole species had been wiped out ... by man

Magellan eagle owls are a vanishing species and don't breed well in captivity, so staff at Tomar Owl Sanctuary in Ashford, Kent were particularly excited when their female owl laid three eggs. Then disaster struck. The mother owl accidentally knocked all three eggs out of the nest. Two were completely smashed and the third was badly cracked. It seemed as if all three of its promised chicks had been lost, but then Tom Tyrell at the sanctuary had a brainwave. Painstakingly he painted over the cracks in the third egg – with Tipp-Ex typewriter correction fluid. Amazingly, it worked – and 34 days later a perfectly healthy Magellan eaglet hatched from the egg. The new arrival, whom the staff called Tipp-Ex, adopted Tom as his father and now joins him on visits to clubs and schools promoting owl conservation.

Bill Britton has taken on one of the hardest jobs any animal rescuer can attempt – re-homing dogs that people wouldn't usually give a second glance. Rather than seeing sick or elderly dogs put to sleep Bill, a disabled American war veteran, saves them from certain death and finds them a new home – somehow. He and his wife Mickie have saved over 1,800 dogs to date from their home in West Jordan, Utah.

'Pets deserve love and care,' says Bill. He convinces families that older dogs aren't 'throwaways' but instead are 'aged to perfection'.

One of his greatest achievements was saving the life of a golden retriever called Mocha. Mocha had been bred in an illegal puppy farm, and had been born without any eyes. The breeders wanted him destroyed, but Bill found him a home with a retired schoolteacher, Owen Wait. 'This dog is the greatest thing that ever happened to me,' Owen says proudly – and he even wears a special T-shirt he's had printed, which reads 'Seeing-Eye Human!'

Australia now has stringent immigration laws that make it virtually impossible for anyone without a visa to get in. But in 1990, one cat succeeded where hundreds of stowaways had failed – by hiding in a car sealed inside a freight container.

It's thought he jumped into the car just as it was being driven into the container at the quayside of Dover docks. No one noticed him there as the heavy doors were closed and the whole container was hoisted aboard.

The journey to Port Adelaide in Southern Australia took over a month but somehow the cat survived without food and water – he may have lapped up condensation that formed on the car windows. He was tired and weak when Australian customs officers found him. Because of Australia's tough anti-rabies laws, the cat should have been put to sleep. However, word spread of his long journey to Australia and Aussie animal lovers besieged the quarantine station offering to pay all of his costs. The authorities gave in and Mercedes (as he was named) was apparently given the 'Rolls-Royce' treatment before finding a new home – with the owner of the car.

It was all too much to bear for Nipper the football-mad dog. There was a minute left on the clock in the hard-fought 1997 Gateshead Derby match between his master's side – the Portland Arms pub team – and their bitter rivals from the Coach and Horses. The score was 4–4. Nipper, a seven-month-old Staffordshire terrier belonging to team captain Steve Wraith, knew he had to do something. He wriggled out of his leash and dashed on to the pitch, tackling the opposing centre-half and scooping the ball from under his feet before heading off towards the goal with it. Three defenders tried to tackle him, but with a series of dazzling body swerves (accompanied by a few threatening growls) he swept by them and flicked the ball across the goal mouth to team striker Gary Roberts who blasted it past the keeper. Everyone looked at the referee, who in turn looked at Nipper. Then he pointed to the halfway line. Goal! 5–4 to Nipper's team! After the final whistle, Nipper joined the team in a lap of honour around the park.

After Nipper's match-winning play, there's talk of him getting a transfer up to the big league – to Blackburn *Rovers* of course!

> The mad poet Byron was incensed to find that he could not keep a dog in his room at Cambridge – so he kept a pet bear instead!

It was the last thing Jonathan Lomas expected to happen when he broke into a house in Houston, Texas. After forcing an entry, he looked up to see 200lbs of porcine fury hurtling at him down the hallway and was immediately knocked flat on his back by the first 'guardpig' he had ever encountered. The pig pinned him there until police arrived. The pig's owner, Rick Charles, had originally bought her to fatten and then eat, but after her heroic act he decided to spare her life.

Each year thousands of dogs go missing and then turn up unexpectedly a day or two later, none the worse for wear. But when Lucas, a dog from South Carolina, disappeared, he caused his owner Earl Cash more than a few sleepless nights, over 1,200 of them, in fact! You see, Lucas turned up more than three and a half years after he went missing in woods near Sudbury in Ontario.

In 1988 Earl was on holiday there with his dog, and on one particular day, they were out hunting. Earl had to keep his wits about him because bears had been seen in the area. Lucas was sniffing about in the forest when he suddenly barked and leapt forward – he'd seen a black bear and was giving chase.

Earl couldn't keep up with him and the dog was soon lost from sight. A few minutes later, though, Earl heard a bear growling and a dog whimpering. He knew that Lucas had been attacked but he didn't know where.

He spent the rest of his week's holiday searching for his dear dog but eventually he gave up, convinced that Lucas must have been killed, and he returned home to South Carolina.

Then, in early 1992, out of the blue, Earl got a call from a lady in the animal control department at Rayside-Balfour, Ontario. A stray dog had been brought in with a tag that identified him as belonging to Earl. Of course, Earl didn't believe her, but when the dog was described he realised it could only be Lucas. It turned out that in the time since he'd gone missing, Lucas had been living wild in the woods, venturing into town to forage for food from dustbins. Amazingly, even after all that time on his own – with all the perils of the forest to contend with – Lucas was remarkably fit, apart from being slightly underweight.

Shortly afterwards, Lucas and Jane Neve, the animal control officer who'd rung Earl, flew down to South Carolina on a trip paid for by a local newspaper.

Lucas and Earl were reunited. As soon as he saw his owner, Lucas literally jumped for joy. After all, three and a half years is a long time to be parted from the one you love.

Terrence Powers of Long Island, New York dropped his old dog Kokomo at his nearby parents' house on Boxing Day 1993. He had to make a trip and the plan was to collect his pet the next day – but when he arrived back, his parents had some bad news. They'd let Kokomo out into the garden late that evening but he hadn't returned.

That night there was a blizzard with temperatures dropping well below freezing. It would be hard for a fit and healthy human to survive, let alone a thirteen-year-old mongrel. The days that followed were just as cold, and thick snow covered the countryside. Terrence and his wife always felt that Kokomo was alive, but after two weeks the chances of finding him were getting more and more remote.

They spent their spare time in January driving around the town asking if anyone had seen Kokomo. To their amazement, during the third week, someone said they thought they'd seen the dog only a few miles away from the Powers' house.

Acting on this tip-off, the Powers decided to change tactics. If *they* couldn't find Kokomo, they'd let him find *them*. That night they slept wrapped in scarves which they took the next day to the approximate spot where the dog was last seen. They then dragged these scarves all the way back to their own house, a few miles away – and waited for Kokomo to pick up their scent.

They didn't have long to wait. A couple of days later, 24 days after Kokomo had disappeared, he turned up on their doorstep, weak and thin but otherwise in good shape.

Murphy, an army donkey, was one of the heroes of Gallipoli, the disastrous attempt by Allied forces to secure the Dardinelles and crush the Turkish forces in 1915. In the battle, repeated advances by British, French and Commonwealth troops were repulsed, with the allies sustaining over 250,000 casualties. Australian and New Zealand troops suffered the most.

Injured soldiers had to make the dangerous trip through 'Shrapnel Gully' to the relative safety of the Turkish beach where they could receive first aid and it was here that Murphy became a war hero. He was trained by John Simpson Kirkpatrick, a twenty-two-year-old stretcher bearer, to help carry the wounded on his back all the way to the field hospitals.

Although Kirkpatrick was killed by a stray bullet, Murphy continued making the perilous journey on his own and many wounded Australians owe their lives to the courageous little donkey.

A statue commemorating Kirkpatrick and Murphy can be seen at the Australian War Memorial. This image of the donkey bowed under the weight of an injured soldier is a powerful reminder of the doomed expedition and the photo used as a basis for the statue is widely reprinted each Anzac Day, Australia's remembrance day. This year Tim Fischer, Australia's deputy Prime Minister, presented the Purple Cross Award posthumously to Murphy on behalf of all the donkeys who saw action at Gallipoli. This award was created by the RSPCA to recognise animal bravery in war. Murphy's courageous action was described as 'one of the great feats of the First World War'.

A cat called Felix must hold the record for the most miles travelled – though not intentionally. She escaped from her box while on a Pan Am flight from Germany in 1988 but searches of the aircraft and airport drew a blank. Her owner, Bill Kubecki, gave up hope of ever seeing Felix again. Meanwhile, that same Felix had been hiding in the luggage hold where she'd made over 60 transatlantic flights, or nearly 180,000 miles. She'd stopped over in New York, Washington, San Francisco and Los

Angeles, jetted down to Rio, Buenos Aires and Santiago and even as far as Riyadh in Saudi Arabia.

It's thought that Felix survived by licking condensation from the hold's walls. She was finally discovered by airline workers at Heathrow Airport but was returned to her owner in the US in much more dignified surroundings – the first-class section.

A Great Dane called Bosley was the guard dog at a scrap yard at Llantrisant in South Wales. He was quite used to the car crusher but one day, just as a wrecked car was about to be squashed into a two-foot cube of compressed metal, Bosley began barking loudly. The yard's owner was about to drop the car into the crusher but he decided to see what was worrying Bosley. The dog had never acted like this before.

Once the machinery had come to a halt Bosley rushed towards the car, sniffing it furiously. On closer examination the owner found a terrified kitten sheltering under one of the front seats and gently removed it.

Thanks to Bosley's keen nose the cat was rescued and found a new home, and a new name – appropriately enough, Lucky.

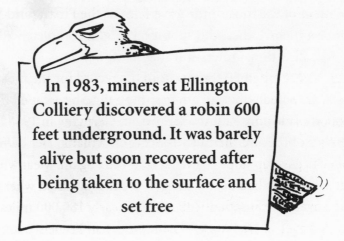

In 1983, miners at Ellington Colliery discovered a robin 600 feet underground. It was barely alive but soon recovered after being taken to the surface and set free

Velia, a German pointer, loved to run. And run. And run. This was the reason her owners gave her away – they just weren't fit enough to keep up with her. Fortunately, the person they gave her to, Mary Goodwin, was an experienced world-class runner. Once she realised how much stamina Velia had, she decided to take the dog running with her. But this wasn't to be a gentle jog or even an energetic cross-country steeplechase – this was the Ultra Run, a gruelling 2,500-mile endurance run in the high altitudes from Nepal to India!

Mary spent half of 1988 training for the race, accompanied by Velia as her 'pacer'. Mary had trouble keeping up, but Velia would bark encouragement back at her to keep her going.

During the actual race, Mary and Velia ran together all the way with a jeep bringing up supplies at the rear. One hundred and seventy days after starting, Mary crossed the finish line – the first woman in the world to complete the race. By her side was Velia – the first dog to do the same!

An Afghan hound race in a greyhound stadium ended in complete anarchy. The daffy dogs didn't have a clue what they were supposed to do and – because of their long shaggy hair – half of the beasts didn't even notice the rabbit when it sped past them. Others did spot it but ran in completely the opposite direction. Others still chased off on more interesting smell trails and, of those who actually did set off after the rabbit, most lost interest or stopped for a toilet break on their way around the track.

On 9 January 1974 the body of an unidentified woman was found near the Kennedy Space Center at Titusville, Florida. For years, detectives searched in vain for the killer – or even clues that might lead them to the killer. Lead after lead was followed up with no results and years went by. Then, in July 1982, the police department received a tip-off about a suspect and he was hauled in for questioning. Although he denied the killing – and any knowledge of the woman – detectives were certain they'd found their man. They just had to prove it.

Harass II was a German shepherd police sniffer dog down at the station, and he was one of the best. On the off-chance that he could help, Harass II was given some clothing worn by the suspect to sniff, and then taken out to the murder spot.

After a short while he picked up a trail – but this led to a completely different site to where the police believed the murder had taken place. They returned to the station with this information and the man they were holding went white. He thought they had irrefutable evidence against him, and made a full confession.

This success was down to the tracking abilities of Harass II, who'd managed to pick up the scent of the murderer over eight and a half years after the incident took place!

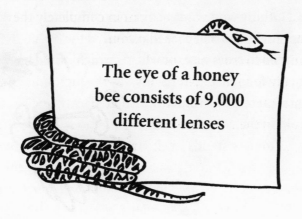

The eye of a honey bee consists of 9,000 different lenses

In February 1939, a steamer set sail from Bootle with a thoroughly miserable crew. They had had to leave without their ship's cat, Sidney James. Sidney hadn't shown up when the ship's siren sounded and now they were off to Buenos Aires, some 5,000 miles away. The journey took weeks, but eventually they arrived – to see Sidney James sitting on the dockside waiting for them. Realising he'd missed his own boat, he'd hopped on board a post boat bound for the same destination and arrived in Buenos Aires six days earlier!

It was January 1925 and Gunnar Kasson had a formidable task ahead of him. He was leading a team of sled dogs transporting supplies of a vital antitoxin to halt a diphtheria epidemic threatening the Alaskan town of Nome. Normally, the drugs would have been flown in but terrible blizzards made this impossible. The only hope of preventing the disease spreading were relay teams of dogs. Gunnar's team was one of a few making the 600-mile journey in some of the worst weather ever seen in Alaska.

Leading the dogs was a black, long-haired malamute called Balto, whose tracking skills didn't desert him even while trekking through blinding blizzards, 80mph winds and sub-zero temperatures. Nothing would divert him from his task, not even having his paws cut by the sharp ice that covered the frozen Bering Sea. Balto managed to cross vast snowdrifts which would have been difficult even for a man to force his way through, and Gunnar's team was the first to enter the isolated town, on 2 February.

A statue of Balto now stands in Central Park, New York in honour of his fantastic feat in delivering the serum safely to Nome. A plaque reads, '*Dedicated to the indomitable spirit of the sled dogs that relayed antitoxin 600 miles over rough ice,*

*treacherous waters, through arctic
blizzards from Nenana to the relief of
stricken Nome in the winter of 1925.
Endurance, Fidelity, Intelligence.'*

Brenda James was visiting her
brother in Manchester
accompanied by her beloved cat,
Cindy. That evening they went out to the theatre, leaving Cindy
at home. When they got back they discovered the house had
been burgled – and Cindy was nowhere to be seen. Brenda was
so heartbroken by the loss that she never replaced Cindy.

After a year and a half, back in West London, she moved house
and about ten months after that a neighbour happened to
mention that she'd seen a half-starved cat sitting on Brenda's
doorstep while she was out. It had looked so thin and pathetic that
she'd taken it in. Brenda could hardly believe her eyes when she
saw the cat. It was Cindy! Brenda had no idea how her cat had
tracked her down from Manchester to London – particularly after
she'd moved house. It seemed like a miracle . . .

Bobbie the collie was the much-loved pet of a restaurant
owner in Silverton, Oregon. On 15 August 1923 Bobbie
and his owner were visiting relatives in Wolcott, Indiana. The
owner had stopped at a petrol station and while he was inside, a
pack of wild dogs chased Bobbie away. By the time his owner
came out, the collie was nowhere to be seen. The owner was
heartbroken, but no amount of searching turned up any clue of
the collie's whereabouts.

Six months later, on 15 February 1924, Bobbie arrived back in
Silverton, Oregon, having completed a journey of some 3,000

miles, successfully crossing the White River, the Wabash River, the Tippecanoe River, the Great Plains and the Rocky Mountains.

He didn't go straight home, though. Instead, he made for the old farmhouse where he had been born and raised. Here, the new farm tenants found him curled up fast asleep on top of the grave of a fox terrier with whom he had been best friends as a pup. After the farmers fed him, Bobbie refused to stay. He continued on to his owner's restaurant and jumped on the bed just as the owner was taking a nap, yapping and licking his face frantically. He was home at last.

Bobbie became a celebrity throughout the United States. Thousands flocked to see the wonder dog. He was awarded a gold collar and several animal medals, as well as being immortalised in Charles Alexander's book, *Bobbie, A Great Collie of Oregon.*

The epic trek seemed to do Bobbie no harm, and he lived on with his owner for another 12 years after coming home.

A jet-setting Siamese cat called Wan Ton made one of the most extraordinary journeys of all time in 1979. He jumped on board a jumbo at Guam in the South Pacific and was later found shivering in the hold of a jet at Heathrow Airport. The London authorities looked at the information on his collar and couldn't believe it. There was no direct plane route between Guam and Heathrow. Wan Ton must have switched planes at Washington, DC!

It's not just cats and dogs who have a fantastic sense of direction. A black bear which was making a nuisance of itself in Michigan was airlifted to a safer spot some 240km away. Within a month or so, the bear had travelled all the way back again. Another group of brown bears in Alaska were also forcibly moved to an area 200km away. Within two months they were all back on their old stomping grounds again!

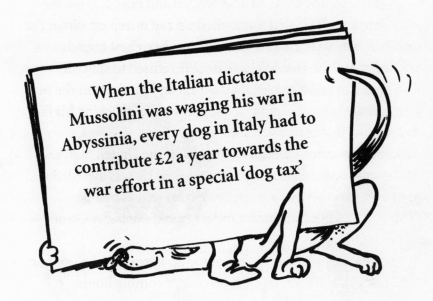

When the Italian dictator Mussolini was waging his war in Abyssinia, every dog in Italy had to contribute £2 a year towards the war effort in a special 'dog tax'

Hedgehogs can do it too. In 1981, Hedgehogs who were moved to Brownsea Island in Poole Harbour always made their way back home again, even if it meant swimming large expanses of water on the way! One European hedgehog is recorded as travelling 48 miles back to its original home in the Ukraine.

The Bristowe family from Monk Bretton, South Yorkshire, were terribly upset when they discovered that Griffin, their seven-month-old black and white cat, had been knocked down and killed by a car. College lecturer Max Bristowe carefully wrapped their beloved pet in a piece of carpet and solemnly buried him in a sunny corner of their garden, watched by his wife Pauline and their three daughters.

The family were distraught at the loss of Griffin so when they heard Pauline cry out from her bedroom, they assumed it was in grief. They rushed in to see if she was all right and there on the bed was Griffin! 'I shouted and everyone rushed upstairs,' said Mrs Bristowe. 'The girls were whooping with delight and couldn't believe it. Griffin just sat there licking himself.'

Then the truth dawned on them. They had buried a different cat – but a cat that looked exactly like Griffin, even to identical black and white markings. The family checked with neighbours but no one had reported a cat missing. They're mystified as to where it came from but, as Mr Bristowe said, 'At least we've given someone else's cat a good send-off.'

The spots on a Holstein cow are completely unique. No two Holsteins ever have the same pattern!

Chapter Two
MONKEY BUSINESS

Basic Instinct was the six to one favourite in the biggest race event of the day at the Atlantic City racetrack. He looked every inch a winner as he was led into the starting gate. Excited spectators jostled for a better view, expecting their horse to romp home. The starting gate sprang open and the horses surged down the field. All of them, that is, except for Basic Instinct. He remained stubbornly in the gate. His jockey, Carlos Barrera, urged him on wildly, but Basic Instinct wasn't going anywhere. They'd shut his tail in the rear stall gate. Furious gamblers were given a refund.

Maybe this is why cockneys call it the 'dog and bone' . . . When Jean Soper left her five-month-old mongrel puppy, Ben, alone while she popped down to the shops, Ben mistook the phone receiver for a nice juicy bone. The poor puppy was teething and it was just too tempting to resist. Ben jumped up, knocked the phone to the floor and started chewing up the receiver. His paw also hit the keys, tapping out 112 – which is the new Europe-wide emergency number, connected to a 999 system. The operator heard heavy breathing and a whimpering sound and alerted the police. The first policewoman on the scene peered through the letterbox and saw the phone lying next to an upturned table – with drops of blood on the floor. Fearing someone had been murdered, she called for back-up. Eight more police officers descended on the house, in Higham, Kent, and proceeded to smash their way in with sledgehammers. They found Ben sitting on his own, the phone receiver in his mouth and his gums bleeding from his enthusiastic teething efforts . . .

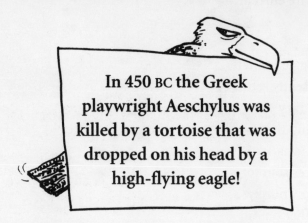

In 450 BC the Greek playwright Aeschylus was killed by a tortoise that was dropped on his head by a high-flying eagle!

It was the most bird-brained blackmail attempt in history. A German supermarket owner was told that, if he didn't pay a criminal gang one million marks, poisoned cartons of yoghurt would find their way on to his shelves. The owner was given instructions to take the money to a disused rubbish tip in the middle of the night. Here he found a crate containing ten homing pigeons each with a tiny hand-sewn rucksack slung over its back. A hastily scribbled note told him to fill the pigeons' rucksacks with the cash and then let them fly free. The owner called in the police. 'We couldn't believe our eyes,' said one detective. 'Each pigeon had a sort of mini sack made of rubber attached to its back with elastic.' But, as the police quickly worked out, the crafty criminals had badly miscalculated. 'A pigeon can only carry about three ounces when it's flying,' the detective pointed out. 'The gang would have needed at least 200 birds. With a million marks on their backs, the poor things would never have made it into the air – they would probably have been flattened!'

A police helicopter was called in and some scraps of paper put into the pigeons' rucksacks before they were freed. The helicopter then followed the pigeons straight back to a farmhouse loft some 30 miles away where the gang was eagerly awaiting their return. The police swooped and now the three-man gang are currently doing 'bird' for their daft scheme.

Moggie Monets, pussy Picassos and tabby Turners are currently setting the art world alight! American collectors are going crazy over paintings made by cats, who pad about in a paintbox and then wipe their paws clean on a canvas. America's highest-paid cat artist, a ginger tom called Bootsie, has his masterpieces sold for up to £50,000. And a group of cat artists – comprising Chunky, Mischief, Rumple, Inky and Smokey – work together on canvases which are then sold for anything up to £38,000!

When it came to showing her political allegiance at the 1997 General Election, Jemimeh the poodle was a dyed-in-the-wool Conservative. Or rather, a dyed-in-the-fur Conservative. To show her and her husband's loyalty to the Conservative Party, Mrs Georgina Wood decided to have Jemimeh – who's normally white – dyed true Tory blue. The only problem was that, when Georgina got home from the pet parlour, her husband was horrified. He'd switched allegiances and was now backing the Referendum Party. He was so disillusioned with his former party that he even refused to take Jemimeh for 'walkies' in case people thought he was a Conservative supporter!

Hille Peartree was stunned. Her twelve-year-old Jack Russell Bella was running an internationally successful company behind her back – and she'd never suspected a thing! She knew that Bella was rather partial to trees, but never guessed she'd developed that interest into building up her own timber company! Hille's suspicions were first raised when Customs and Excise first wrote to Bella at 'Bella Ltd' demanding that she fill in a VAT registration form. Then another VAT registration form arrived, followed by a list of European business sales contacts and a VAT return to send back. It took several long phone calls to her local Customs and Excise office to convict officials that her dog wasn't running a company. At first, the VAT men were adamant that Bella was indeed a captain of industry and would pay up or else – until they discovered a clerical error, and a million to one coincidence. There was a company called Bella Ltd, and it had a very similar address to Mrs Peartree's home in Capel St Mary near Ipswich.

I'm not spinning you a yarn. There's a new knitting craze – using dog hair instead of wool. As you might expect, the craze started in America, with the publication of a book called *Knitting with Dog Hair* which included new and exciting knitting patterns for everything 'from a golden retriever scarf to a glamorous sweater from your Samoyed'. It's also available in the UK. As the publisher says: 'Better the sweater from the dog you know and love than from the sheep you'll never meet!'

Hoaxers got hundreds of kindly old ladies knitting 'birdigans' – cardigans made for birds after an oil spill in the Shetlands. They were told to make them 'gaily coloured' so that the birds would like them and to leave little arm holes for their wings. A Scottish RSPCA officer dismissed the hoax – and the idea of 'birdigans': 'They'll unbalance the birds,' she said, 'because they're not used to wearing coats and they'll fall over . . .'

Koala bears have found themselves the prime suspects in many house burglaries throughout Australia in recent years. Don't worry though, the lovable bears aren't turning delinquent. It's just that their fingerprints are almost exactly like human ones. They have the same pattern of swirls on their dabs as we do. Apparently this helps them climb their favourite eucalyptus trees better. And with more koalas coming to live in the suburbs of capital cities, their fingerprints keep getting found at crime scenes!

Mice actually sing. However, they sound pretty awful so it's a good thing that their singing voices are pitched far too high for the human ear to register!

A Welsh farmer had a very special collie. Not only could it herd sheep, it could also count them. It did this by barking as the farmer counted aloud. If the collie stopped barking after, say, ten, then there were ten sheep in the field – and so on. The dog was always right. On one occasion, the farmer asked his dog to run over to a field and count the sheep. He knew there were 25 there.

Then he began counting. To his astonishment, the collie stopped barking after 24. The farmer counted again: and again his dog stopped barking after '24' was called out.

The dog had never got it wrong, so the farmer went into the field to check. Sure enough, there were 24. The 25th had escaped through a damaged gate and was later found wandering in a lane.

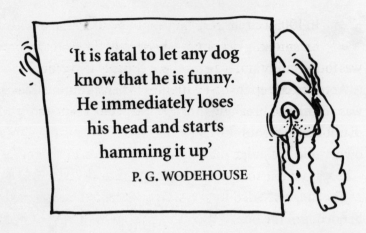

'It is fatal to let any dog know that he is funny. He immediately loses his head and starts hamming it up'

P. G. WODEHOUSE

A British army officer was on official duty in Paris, which meant he had to wear his ceremonial dress uniform. Walking along a street one day he was accosted by a stray dog. It ran up to him and before he had a chance to shoo it away, it had wiped its muddy paws all over his best shiny boots. Fortunately there was a shoe-shine stall up ahead and in minutes he looked as smart as ever.

Later that week the officer was on the same street when the same muddy dog dirtied his boots. And once again, he had to get them polished by the shoe-shine. He thought this was too much of a coincidence and after he watched the street for a while, all was revealed. The dog belonged to the shoe-shine, who had trained him to muddy the shoes of passers-by – a very cunning trick to increase business!

A New Zealand hunter was determined to bag a duck for his supper but the duck he was shooting at was determined not to be that meal. Going into a steep dive, it hit the hunter square in the face, leaving him with broken glasses and a broken nose. Recovering from the impact the duck in question composed itself and then flew off, none the worse for the collision.

In 1905 a circus chimp in South Bend, Indiana, was arrested for smoking in public – a criminal offence at the time. He was found guilty and his owner was ordered to pay his fine.

Another chimp involved in monkey business was Makao, who was accused of breaking into a French apartment and stealing a diamond ring from the owner's jewellery box. In court Makao's owner told the judge that his monkey couldn't possibly be guilty – he was unable to open a jewellery box as described.

The judge decided to put Makao to the test and a court ushers handed him the box in question. Makao took hold of it, sniffed it, turned it around in his hands – then promptly opened it. His owner had to pay for the missing ring.

Just like birds,
gibbons sing a
dawn chorus

Thurlow Craig, a newspaper reporter, recalled an incident described to him by an old prospector he'd interviewed. The man lived in a remote log cabin with his three cats for company.

It seemed that he got fed up with the cats leaping up on to his chair as soon as he'd vacated it so he rigged up a sort of booby trap to discourage them. What he did was cut the chair seat in half, hinging both halves from the sides. He covered each bit with half a cushion and fitted a bolt under the middle that kept the two halves firmly together.

He then rigged up a lever in the cabin which connected to the bolt with a cable. If he got up and a cat decided to take his place then he'd just move the lever and the chair would split in two, depositing the cat unceremoniously on to the cabin floor. He would then re-set the chair and take his place once more.

The prospector knew it was far easier to just lift the cats off his chair but he wanted a real way of discouraging them. The cats soon learned what would happen if they dared take their master's chair, but one day the laugh was on him. He was sitting down and the cats must have figured what to do because they managed to push the lever themselves. The seat parted and he ended up trapped in the chair frame. He had to use his bowie knife to cut his way out.

After that he rebuilt the chair – with a solid seat once more.

Private Jackie was the strangest looking soldier in the 3rd South African Infantry Regiment – and certainly the shortest. Debate still rages about whether or not he was the ugliest. Private Jackie was a baboon. He'd joined up with his owner, Albert Marr, and soon made a home for himself at the barracks. His fellow soldiers made him a smart little uniform to wear, and he'd strut about the parade ground saluting any officer he saw. He also lit cigarettes for his fellow troopers and excelled at guard duty.

When the First World War began, Private Jackie was posted to Europe along with Albert and was issued with his own rations and pay book. He soon saw action against both the Turks and the Germans. When Albert was wounded at the battle of Agagia in 1916, Private Jackie stayed with him, comforting him and hugging him as bullets flew all around their position. Private Jackie was wounded too, at the battle of Passchendaele, but recovered and received a medal for his bravery, along with promotion to corporal. At the end of the war, Corporal Jackie paraded in the Lord Mayor's procession through London with the rest of the war heroes, sitting astride a cannon barrel and saluting everyone fit to bust!

A performing troupe of pit bull terriers missed their opening night at the 1991 Edinburgh Festival when they were seized by customs officers at Dover. The group, called 'Crufts on Acid', were about to embark on a sell-out tour of Europe. 'They are lovely, frisky dogs,' said promoter Michael Gilmore, then added, rather defensively, 'and all of them have been through a course of therapy at the Chicago Dangerous Dogs Retraining Centre . . .'

When the heron is fishing it raises its wings around its head like a sunshade. This enables it to see into the water much more clearly

The manager of an engineering company near Goa came back to his office one day in 1987 to find that it had been taken over – not by disgruntled workers staging a sit-in, but by a large, hissing cobra.

Since many Hindus feel the cobra is sacred, religious leaders were consulted about what action should be taken. After much deliberation, they informed the manager that the snake must not be disturbed – especially by loud noises from the factory. The result was that the plant had to shut down while anxious workers and management waited for the snake to leave. It finally did move off – three months later!

In 1988 Fred Ringgenburg of Hemet in California was issued with a MasterCard credit card with $5,000 worth of credit. Nothing unusual in that – except that Fred was a tomcat belonging to Janet Ringgenburg!

Farmer Mark Purdey of Exmoor plays the flute and the saxophone to his 70 Jersey cows. It makes them produce more milk apparently. 'The cows really enjoy the flute,' Mark says, 'but the bull seems to prefer the sax!'

Poor Brucie the marabou stork was finding it hard to attract a mate. The only male in Colchester Zoo's colony, Brucie had lost part of his lower beak in an accident and it was

harming his chatting-up technique. Female marabou storks
don't respond to sweet nothings as much as they do to loud
clacking noises made by the male's beak during courtship – and
Brucie was getting the cold shoulder. In desperation, keepers
turned to a local dentist who fitted Brucie with a false beak. The
job was done so skilfully that Brucie was soon able to make
precisely the right noises again and won his girlfriends back.

In April 1996, Liverpool University played host to a
historic first – Britain's first pet pig show! Prized pet
porkers gathered from all over the country to compete in beauty
contests, obedience trials and even a competition to see who
could play a musical instrument the best!

Bimbo was a rhesus monkey brought to Chessington Zoo
from Africa in August 1966. She arrived on board a flight
to Heathrow but as soon as she landed, she started her monkey
business. While keepers were distracted for a moment she
scampered off, ran across the tarmac and straight into a BOAC
hangar where she disappeared up in the high rafters, swinging
from beam to beam. Bimbo's 'Great Escape' lasted 204 days
before she was lured down by the zoo authorities.

She settled down at the zoo, but not for long. Less than two
years later she escaped once more and turned Chessington Zoo
upside down as she raced all over the place with a team of out-
of-breath keepers lagging sadly behind. It took the entire zoo
staff to track her down and get her back.

Safely behind bars once more, Bimbo gave birth to two baby
rhesus monkeys who inherited their mother's taste for adventure.
On several occasions Bimbo had to prevent them from escaping –
you could say they were just aping their mother!

The University of Colorado's football team had a mascot called Ralphie – a 1,000lb American bison. From 1963 to 1978, Ralphie (a female bison) made rousing appearances at Folsom Field in Boulder, inspiring the home team to victory by running the length of the field, turning round, and thundering back again to her trailer. On one occasion Ralphie forgot to stop and just kept running round the pitch. In an attempt to stop her the scoreboard flashed the message 'Ralphie Come Home'. Ralphie's successor is Ralphie II, who's a little heavier: 1,400lbs.

When Buster the hamster got the urge to hit the road he certainly did it in style!

His owner, seven-year-old Stephanie Dawson, had put Buster in his bright yellow exercise ball and left him peddling away in the garden of her home in Ipswich, Suffolk, while she cleaned his cage.

In his enthusiasm, Buster pedalled so hard on the little wheel inside the ball that he actually got it rolling – and then he was off! Still pedalling furiously, Buster propelled himself out of the garden, through the front gate and off the pavement – joining the traffic on the busy road outside. Drivers swerved in all directions as the hamster pedalled his ball down the middle of the road, with no regard whatsoever for the Highway Code! Luckily one driver stopped and picked him up before he could cause any more mayhem. Buster was deposited with a nearby vet and reunited with his owner two days later after she'd put a notice in a nearby newsagent's asking if anyone had spotted her hamster. Stephanie was delighted to get him back but gave him a stern talking-to. 'I've told him not to play hide-and-seek with me again,' she said.

Chapter Three

HOME IS WHERE
THE HEART IS

He broke the hearts of a nation – a little grey and white scruffbag of a dog callously dumped by his owner on a platform at Charing Cross Station. His master had put a pair of old boots down and told his faithful dog to stay and guard them – and then simply walked away. The dog was torn between guarding the boots and following his master but, obedient to the last, he stayed and did his duty. With his master gone, there was no way the dog would let anyone near those precious boots, and it took a policeman with a rope tied to a pole to finally restrain him and take him off to Battersea Dogs Home. The precious boots went with him, and the staff named him 'Bootsie'. Bootsie's story spread and a *Daily Mirror* photographer went down to Battersea to photograph him holding the boots – all he had left of his beloved master – in his mouth. The editor of the *Mirror* cleared the middle pages of the paper and devoted them to Bootsie and his sad story. The very next day, over 700 readers from all over the country called up eager to offer the faithful and devoted dog a new home. In the end, he was adopted by a hairdresser from Bristol who lived above her salon. It meant that Bootsie could be with her all day – and would never have to be alone again.

For 27 years, Inga and Raja the Indian elephants lived together in Dushanbe Zoo in the former Soviet province of Tadjikistan. Keepers said they were inseparable. Then, tragically, Inga developed lung complications after a severe cold and died. Inga's death devastated Raja. As keepers watched, he dropped to his knees beside her with tears streaming down his face and could not be coaxed from her side. Zoo workers tried to remove Inga's body by crane, but Raja wouldn't stand for it. He grabbed the ropes in his trunk and ripped them to shreds. Keepers trying to enter the enclosure were warned off in no uncertain terms. For one day and night, Raja stood guard over his dead companion and then his mourning seemed to end. He allowed the keepers gently to remove Inga's body, and even helped them to do so.

A similar thing happened at Colchester Zoo in 1985, when an African elephant called Moto died suddenly. For five hours her best friend Toto stood by her side, trying to revive her, caressing her with her trunk and pushing at her, encouraging her to get up and allowing no one near. Then, all at once she seemed to accept that her friend was gone and allowed keepers to come in to take the body.

When Richard and Jenny King of New York got divorced, the judge awarded each of them custody of one of their two Labradors. But – concerned that the dogs might miss each other more than their owners would – the animal-loving judge instructed that the two dogs should be allowed to see each other every Sunday!

When the Sydney dog shelter she worked at became overcrowded with strays and waifs, volunteer Janet Bryant hit upon a novel solution. She started 'marrying' the dogs to each other and then suggesting that prospective owners adopt a couple rather than just one dog. It worked, and adoptions at the centre doubled. Now Janet has a thriving business outside the shelter for owners who want their dogs to do the right thing. For £400, she'll marry your dog and the partner of his or her choice, supplying wedding gowns and tuxedos, a wedding certificate, a catered reception and even a honeymoon suite. Before you think she's barking mad, Janet reckons she officiates at over 150 canine weddings every year!

A troop of 40 hedgehogs presented a petition to parliament! They turned up at the House of Commons to present the 35,000 signature petition at the invitation of Robert Jones, MP for Hertfordshire West. The petition called for full legal protection for the hedgehog and was organised by St Tiggywinkles, the specialist hedgehog hospital in Aylesbury

Dodger the beagle was out on a rabbit-hunting trip with his master when he was unlucky enough to fall foul of an overly mothering black bear. Sniffing around for rabbits in the freezing cold, he wandered into the bear's den, found it nice and snug and curled up for 40 winks – not realising he was cuddling

up to a mama brown bear and her two four-week-old cubs.
While Dodger was asleep, he got covered in bear scent and,
when the mama bear awoke, she took him to be one of her cubs.
Every time Dodger tried to leave, mama bear dragged him back
– and gave him a clip round the head for good measure.

After a day's searching the wilderness around Wilton, Maine,
Dodger's owner Butch McCormick stumbled past the den
calling the dog's name. Dodger rushed out to greet his master,
but the she-bear was even quicker, grabbing his back legs and
dragging the hapless beagle back in again. Butch fled, but
returned several days later with state game wardens who finally
managed to extricate the beagle after what was described as 'a
gentle tug of war' with the she-bear. The three-year-old beagle
was none the worse for wear. Indeed he'd apparently quite
enjoyed his stay, and hadn't gone hungry. The mama bear had
suckled him along with her cubs.

Shep the dog never forgot his master's last command –
and he obeyed it until he died. Shep's master, Francis
McMahon, was rushed to a nearby hospital after falling down a
flight of stairs. Shep tagged along with his family and waited
anxiously for news. At first, Francis seemed to be making a good
recovery. As he was wheeled out of the operating theatre, he saw
Shep and asked the porter to stop. He reassured his dog that
everything was all right now and that Shep should wait for him.
But, tragically, Francis's condition deteriorated and he died just
a few hours later. At the moment Francis passed away, his family
said Shep let out a howl of utter despair and then began to bark
in distress. At every opportunity from then on, Shep would
escape from the family home and go racing down to the hospital
to wait. This carried on for 12 years, until the faithful old dog
died.

A cat named Barney wandered on to a building site at North Tawton in Devon and somehow got lost in the maze of sewage pipes that were being laid to a new housing development. His owner, Gill Tregunna had given Barney up for lost but was relieved 13 days later when an astonished plumber saw a cat's head pop up in a toilet bowl in one of the houses being built!

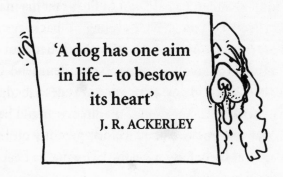

'A dog has one aim in life – to bestow its heart'
J. R. ACKERLEY

Pud the collie is a mum with a difference – she brought up three puppies and two piglets! Pud lived on a farm near Carlisle where one of the sows gave birth to 18 piglets. Two of these seemed to have a natural affinity with Pud rather than their mother and were soon being suckled and reared by her. Now, the piglets get on well with Pud's real puppies and even try to act like dogs – although their attempts to sit up and beg on their hind legs aren't very successful.

If there was a prize for 'Pet Persistence' then it would surely go to a Persian cat named BC. He lived in the town of Palmerston North in New Zealand with his owner Marjorie Cummerfield but when she moved two miles away, he decided he was homesick. BC was so homesick in fact, that he ran away back to his old house nearly 80 times. It might have been only two miles away but each time BC managed to successfully cross four main roads and many minor ones on the way, before being taken back, once again, to Marjorie's new home.

The bond between a guide dog and its master is one of the strongest ties there can be. For years, Canelo faithfully guided his blind diabetic master to and from his local hospital in Cadiz, Spain for treatment. Canelo would be left tethered at the entrance and collected on his master's return. Then one day, his master never came back out. He had suffered a heart attack and died. Canelo refused to leave, sitting perfectly still outside the hospital entrance night and day. Patients and staff brought him food and played with him, but then someone reported Canelo as a stray and he was unceremoniously rounded up and bundled into the local animal shelter. By now, the story of Canelo's devotion was well known in the area. Local people paid to have him freed from the shelter and allowed to return to the hospital grounds. Canelo is still there to this day. Although he sometimes takes a stroll to stretch his legs, or collect his free daily dinner from a nearby restaurant, he always returns to wait by the hospital entrance, still hoping against hope that his master will one day reappear.

Trapped in the middle of the London Blitz, a sweet tabby cat called Faith sheltered her baby kitten, Panda, with her own body as masonry crashed down all about them. The mother had taken her kitten into St Augustine's Church in the city and had scouted out the way down to the crypt, where she seemed to know she and her baby would be safest. The two were found in the bombed-out church by the Vicar the next day as he searched the ruins. They were dusty and trembling, but unhurt. For her selfless devotion, Faith was awarded a silver medal and a certificate by the PDSA. You can still see a picture of Faith, and her certificates, hung proudly in the church, next to an inscription telling the full story of Faith's devotion. It reads:

'Our dear little church cat, the bravest cat in all the world. On Monday September 9 1940, she endured perils and horrors beyond the power of words to tell. Shielding her kitten in a sort of recess (a spot she selected three days before the tragedy occurred) she sat through the whole frightful night of bombing and fire, guarding her little kitten.

The roof and masonry exploded. The whole house blazed. Floors fell through in front of her. Fire and water and ruin were all around her. Yet she stayed calm and steadfast, and waited for help. We rescued her in the early morning, while the place was still burning, and by the mercy of the Almighty God, she and her kitten were not only saved, but unhurt. God be praised and thanked for his goodness and mercy to our little pet.'

In 1985, a mum-to-be cat with a definite identity crisis climbed a 15-foot-high tree on a farm near Bradwell in Derbyshire and gave birth to three healthy kittens in an abandoned magpie's nest!

A collie named Cindy Loo seemed to sense whenever any of her family were in danger. On one occasion her mistress was late home and Cindy suddenly began to howl. She didn't seem hurt so her owner, Mr Morgan, opened the door to let her out. Cindy refused to leave. Then the telephone rang. It was Mrs Morgan, but before she could speak, her husband asked her if she'd had a car accident. She had – although she was all right. This was just one example of Cindy's 'second sight'.

Years later, Mr Morgan was ill in hospital and his wife and stepson John were in the lounge with Cindy. At exactly ten minutes past ten, Cindy perked up and licked first Mrs Morgan's face and then John's. She then tilted her head back and gave a long, mournful howl.

This was interrupted by the phone ringing. It was the hospital saying that Mr Morgan had just died.

A Hucknall ambulance was out of service for five weeks so a blackbird could hatch four eggs under its bonnet

A Labrador named Toffee has a most unlikely friend – a dolphin called Jo-Jo. The two met in the West Indies where Toffee was out in the boat of his owner, Kevin Roche. They saw the dolphin following the boat and before Kevin knew it, Toffee had jumped overboard and was frolicking in the sea with his new-found pal.

The two animals have met regularly since then. When Jo-Jo sees Toffee in the boat she leaps into the air. This is the signal for Toffee to jump overboard again. In the water they splash and chase each other until Kevin decides it's time to return to the dock.

Both animals then rub nozzles as if to say goodbye – and wait eagerly for their next meeting.

Margaret Adams was distraught when her cat Sampson went missing during a caravan holiday in Wales. She asked shopkeepers and villagers if they'd seen him, advertised in the local newspaper and enquired at police stations for miles around, but no one could help.

Resigned that Sampson wouldn't be coming back, Mrs Adams began her return journey to her home in Plaistow, East London. Two years later, she was in her garden when she noticed a bedraggled-looking cat sitting on the wall. At first she didn't recognise him, but the distinctive markings meant that this could only be her lost cat. She called his name and Sampson jumped down, grateful to be back. He'd travelled 250 miles from South Wales at the leisurely pace of a third of a mile each day.

A pig that thinks she's a cat lives in Maria Hennessey's animal sanctuary in South Wales. The pig in question shares her cats' litter tray, their food and even curls up beside them in front of the fire!

When the Ylonen family found Hubert the elk, he was just a tiny little baby, sheltering by his mother's side. He couldn't understand that she had been hit and killed by a car. The Finnish family took him home, and soon found themselves with a fully grown elk as a pet! Officially, he was to live in the garden shed but the Ylonens only had to leave the back door ajar and he'd be inside, up the stairs and fast asleep on the bed! Hubert was so tame that he'd willingly allow the family's three-year-old daughter to ride on his back and would happily walk around the garden with the family cat clinging to him. However, before you get any ideas about having an elk as a pet, the Ylonens say that pet elks are incredibly clumsy and destructive. They're also absolutely impossible to toilet train – and this is rather a large animal we're talking about here. Better to stick to a budgie!

During the Second World War Fido, an Italian mongrel, lived with his owner in Borgo San Lorenzo, a village just outside of Florence. Every evening at exactly the same time, Fido would trot into town to wait at the bus stop for his master's return from work. One day, however, Fido's master was tragically killed at work during a bombing raid.

When his beloved master failed to get off the bus that evening, Fido refused to give up hope that he would return. Every day for the next 15 years, at precisely the same time, Fido would wait at the bus stop to look at the passengers' faces – just in case his master was among them. He would wait until the last passenger had got off and then trot homewards with his head hung low . . .

A few years later the villagers put up a plaque in honour of their favourite little dog and the mayor was to present him with a specially struck gold medal in honour of his devotion. He was just about to hang the medal around Fido's neck when the dog ran off . . . it was time to meet the bus.

A dachshund named Mr Chips stepped in to help rear an animal rejected by its mother at a zoo in Southport. The creature in question – a tiger

A British official in upper Egypt at the turn of the century always used to take his bull terrier, Peter, with him on the train journey when he had business in Cairo. The journey lasted some 15 hours and Peter seemed bored by it. When his master was transferred to Demanhour, on the other side of Cairo, he decided to travel into Cairo on his own for once, leaving Peter behind with his servants.

As you might expect, Peter had other ideas. He jumped on the train for Cairo to look for his master. When he got to Cairo, he changed platforms, changed trains and set off back on the 15-hour journey to upper Egypt. Not finding his master there, he got back on the train, spent another 15 hours travelling down to

Cairo and then toured the city visiting several of his master's friends! When there was still no sign of his master, Peter jumped back on the train for Demanhour and found that his master had returned some time earlier . . .

 A car wash at a garage in Halesworth in Suffolk is home to a blackbird – who doesn't seem to mind getting a bath up to 70 times a day. The bird built her nest on top of one of the electric motors and while she's patiently sitting on her four eggs, seems impervious to the brightly coloured brushes whirling 18 inches away, and the soapy water spraying in her direction. The garage owners are keeping a careful watch on the blackbird and have asked motorists not to use the hot air driers, since they ruffle her feathers.

Chapter Four
A HELPING PAW

Grant and Danna Easton bid $300 at an auction to raise much-needed funds for Marine World's Elephant Encounter in Vallejo, California. Their reward – a car wash from a four and a half ton elephant called Judy! Following her keeper's instructions, Judy gently sponged down the Eastons' Ford Taurus and then just as delicately dried it off with a towel. She finished off her five-star valeting service by hoovering out the insides of the car with her trunk, apparently leaving the car looking like new!

A British Airways jumbo jet made an emergency landing – to save the life of a dog. BA flight 224 was two hours out of Logan Airport, Boston over the Atlantic on its way to Gatwick when pilot Captain Rex Graveley noticed that the heating had failed in the cargo hold. He knew that down in the hold was a five-year-old Tibetan shih-tzu called Louise, and that the temperature down there was now well below zero. If he did nothing, Louise would certainly die, but if he turned back it would cost British Airways £20,000 and considerably inconvenience all 200 passengers on board. Captain Graveley went on the cabin speakers and explained the situation. The response from the passengers was unanimous – turn back!

'There really was no hesitation,' says Captain Graveley, who owns a springer spaniel himself. 'Everyone from top executives to backpackers jumped to the defence of the dog!'

The plane headed back to Boston and raced to make an emergency landing. Louise was met off the flight by a veterinary surgeon standing by on the runway, who confirmed that her condition was not serious.

Louise's owner, Irene Saunders, was on board the plane and was thrilled by the actions of the flight crew and the passengers. 'They saved her life and I will be eternally grateful,' she says. 'When I saw Louise's little face come out of the cargo hold I wanted to kiss every single passenger and member of the crew for what they had done. Louise is like my little child. She is my family and means everything to me.'

Captain Graveley and his crew were later honoured for their actions by the World Society for the Protection of Animals.

Squirrels in Ryde on the Isle of Wight are having a swinging time learning road safety! Caring locals have built them a rope bridge, high enough above a busy road for them to scamper from one side to the other in perfect safety.

Phyllis Millar's faithful old Dalmatian, Tarily, helped save Mrs Millar's life when she fell and dislocated her hip while out walking in deserted woodlands near her home in Mannings Heath, Sussex. Trapped there, she blew a whistle which she always carried for safety, but no one came to her help. Hours passed with no sign of anyone. Tarily cuddled up to her mistress, comforting her and keeping her warm through her ordeal. Meanwhile, her son Jason came out looking for her. At one point he must have passed within 20 yards of his mother, but didn't see her through the thick undergrowth. In the end, he alerted the police and they scrambled a search helicopter. Almost immediately the helicopter crew spotted Tarily's distinctive black and white spots down below and winched Mrs Millar away to hospital. Tarily was allowed to go and visit her later. 'Tarily would not leave me alone although I tried to send her home,' Mrs Millar said later. 'She is a very good dog and saved my life by staying with me.' Despite her loyalty though, Tarily did not receive any extra dog biscuits as a reward. 'She's too fat already,' Mrs Millar said.

There are 2,292 animals on the payroll of the British Army at the moment. As you might expect, the majority are dogs and horses but the list also includes two goats, a ram, an antelope and a ferret!

An incredible 500,000 cats served officially with the British Army during the Great War. They were employed to keep down the mice and rat population in the trenches. During the Second World War, the Ministry of Supply organised a special call-up for cats, requiring them to fight not the Germans, but armies of mice and rats that threatened Britain's top secret food dumps.

Owners wishing to donate their pets to the war effort were advised to take them along to their nearest pet shop, where they were given between two and five shillings each. The Minister of

Food ruled that 'all cats engaged in work of national importance should receive an official powdered milk ration'! Just after the war, when food was still in short supply all over Europe, the Americans began a special Lease-Lend moggie scheme! Called Cats for Europe, the scheme shipped thousands of prime pussies over the Atlantic to help guard warehouses and grain silos. Ironically, it had been Europe that had first introduced cats to America in the mid eighteenth century – to help the Americans guard *their* foodstocks.

There have been few police officers as dedicated or as keen as Dox, a German shepherd who served with the Italian police force in the 1950s. He was the scourge of the criminal underworld. By the time he was fourteen he had won numerous awards for valour and had been wounded seven times. On one occasion, he personally rounded up a 12-strong gang and herded them up against a wall, keeping them there until help arrived. During his long and distinguished career he also saved a child from being run over and caught a dangerous burglar after a three-mile chase, despite having been shot in the leg. But perhaps Dox's greatest crime-busting achievement came towards the end of his life. He was out on routine patrol with his handler when a man passed him in the street. His handler didn't recognise the man as a criminal who'd given them the slip in a chase six months earlier – but Dox did. The fearless German shepherd turned and pounced on him and stood over the hapless criminal, pinning him down. He wasn't getting away from Dox twice!

When Paula and Stanley Wiggs arrived home from hospital with their newborn son Keith, they seriously considered getting rid of their white Persian cat, Snowball. The couple, from Akron, Ohio, had heard the old wives' tales of cats smothering babies and were worried about their son's safety. They couldn't have been more wrong. One day, when Keith was nine months old, Paula was downstairs in her kitchen when she heard Snowball start up an almighty screeching from upstairs. She yelled at him to be quiet, he'd wake the baby. Snowball didn't listen. His howling grew wilder, louder and more insistent. Paula stormed upstairs to give him a stern telling off – and realised to her horror that the noises were coming from inside the nursery. Little Keith had somehow pulled his mobile down into his cot and the strings had got trapped around his neck and were slowly suffocating him. Paula sliced through the strings with a pair of nail clippers and scooped her son up into her arms. He was crying now and gasping, shocked and scared but safe in his mother's arms. Snowball jumped up on to the cot rail and began to rub himself against them both to share in their relief. 'Snowball was a true hero. He saved our son's life,' Paula said later.

Keith's father made Snowball a special 'lifesaver' badge for his collar, and there has been no more talk of getting rid of him.

In America's prestigious Talamore golf course at Pinehurst in North Carolina, llamas are being trained as golf caddies! Apparently, they can make excellent caddies – although they stop short of offering advice on which iron to use. The design of their hooves means that their weight is evenly spread, so they don't ruin the grass. However, I haven't heard of any British golf clubs who will recognise them yet – and it will probably be a very long time before we see Gleneagles renamed Glenllamas!

Guide dogs are incredible enough, when you think of their extraordinary skill and caring – but is the world ready for the coming of the 'Guide Cow'? Strangers visiting Hartsville, Tennessee would have been shocked to see the local vicar, the Reverend O. F. Robertson, being led everywhere by his cow, Mary. The Reverend hadn't trained Mary in any way. The whole thing was her idea. Realising that the Reverend's eyesight was failing, she started to guide him around his farmstead with gentle nudges of her muzzle. After a while, the two became inseparable, and Mary accompanied him into town, helping to bring him back safely every time.

Racing pigeons were used in the original Olympic Games to carry the results to outlying villages

The construction of America's Grand Coulee Dam could not have been completed without the help of a cat, who succeeded where scores of trained engineers failed. The problem was trying to feed a steel cable through a conduit. The engineers had tried several methods without success. Then one of them noticed how a stray cat was inquisitively sniffing around the end of the open channel. They tied a piece of string to its tail and watched it disappear into the winding conduit before emerging a few minutes later out the other end. Once the string was through they attached a rope to this and the cable to the rope – and the problem was solved!

During the English Civil War, King Charles I's army was laying siege to the city of Gloucester. The people were desperately short of food and unable to last more than a few days when the civic leaders had a plan. There was one pig remaining in the city and it was released just within the perimeter walls. So glad was it of its freedom, that this one little pig squealed all the way round the city. The king, hearing the commotion, imagined a city full of healthy pigs and ample stores for the citizens to continue holding out against him – so he abandoned the siege.

'While the cat's away –
the house smells better'

ANON

The usual hazards faced by city guide dogs include cars, kerbs and pedestrians – not fallen trees, rocks and streams – but that's what a German shepherd called Orient had to contend with. Orient belonged to Bill Irwin, who decided one day that it would be interesting to go on a hike – 2,100 miles along the Appalachian Trail.

The two of them set out in March 1990 from Bill's home in Georgia; both were wearing backpacks filled with supplies for their mammoth 'walkies'.

The incredible journey took them through extremes of temperature, along mountain paths, and had them contending with thick mud, heavy downpours and biting winds. Eventually, after eight arduous months, Orient and Bill arrived exhausted at the end of the trail. Bill could not praise his guide dog strongly enough – Orient had kept him out of danger every step of the way. 'He was my compass and my companion,' he told waiting well-wishers.

Blackie had been Jim O'Brien's guide dog for over 12 years before she herself started to go blind. Jim obviously had to have a new dog, but couldn't bear to be parted from her. The solution? Give Blackie her own guide dog.

Help arrived in the form of another Labrador, Cresta, and the three of them out together were a popular sight in Jim's home town of Market Harborough.

The cat with the worst job in the whole world must have been Minstrel. He was based at the Metropolitan Police Training Centre in Kent and his task for nearly ten years was to nonchalantly stroll past a line of huge slobbering German shepherd police dogs to test their discipline.

The concern wasn't that one of the dogs might have broken ranks and chased Minstrel – but that this unruly behaviour might have encouraged all the other dogs to join in. Fortunately, the police dog handlers do an excellent job and Minstrel didn't once have to worry.

They say that Mounties always get their man – well so did Major, a police dog who chased a suspected burglar after he had managed to give Welsh police the slip in 1983. To make his escape the man climbed up a 100-foot quarry face, swam a river and crashed through thick undergrowth to get to the outskirts of a village.

Hours later, police eventually found not the burglar, but Major – looking the worse for wear. He was sitting by the front door of a house. His handler wanted to take him home but Major wouldn't budge. On the off-chance, the police got a search warrant but couldn't find anything in the house – or anyone. Still Major wouldn't move, so at last his handler let him in the house. There he found the burglar – hiding in a wardrobe.

In the fens of East Anglia, cats were kept to warn of impending floods. If the family cat insisted on going upstairs to sleep, or climbed on top of shelves or cupboards, it was taken as a sure sign that flood waters were on the way

Peanuts the cat was one of Romford Council's cheapest employees in the 1960s. As their official rat catcher he was paid two pints of milk and four cans of cat food per week.

Candy, the rat catcher employed by Bradford City Council in 1984, was responsible for an inter-union squabble and nearly caused a walkout! It started when she became a member of Nalgo (The National and Local Government Officers' Association) but after a short while, some of her union brothers were up in arms, claiming that since she had a manual trade, she shouldn't have been allowed to join a white-collar union (actually, I think her collar was a red felt one with a little bell).

Fortunately, NUPE (the National Association of Public Employees) agreed to take her on and industrial action was averted.

The Angel Memorial Hospital in Boston carries out hundreds of life-saving blood transfusions every year – on animals. Pets who donate blood are given the equivalent of tea and a biscuit afterwards – in this case it's pet treats.

> 'Cats know how to obtain food without labour, shelter without confinement and love without penalties'
>
> W. L. GEORGE

Darts players at the Black Swan pub in Newcastle used to be assisted by Kitty, a cat who learned to jump up at the dartboard, knock the darts out with her paws and take them back to the players in her mouth!

Lita Nahas of Cairo runs the most unusual window-cleaning business in the world – all her employees are camels. 'I just mix sugar with the soap,' she explains. 'I put it on the windows and the camels lick it off. We can do an entire ground floor in minutes.'

Schoolboy Wayne Norgate loved the sea and sailing in his little five-foot dinghy. On one such occasion in 1988 he was out in shallow waters around Mablethorpe in Lincolnshire while on holiday with his parents. Before he knew it, freak currents had carried him out into the North Sea. No matter how hard he paddled, he was getting further and further away from the shore. Wayne was by now extremely frightened and about a mile from the beach.

Suddenly he felt the dinghy shift and feared that it might capsize. He was reassured, though, when he turned around and saw a seal swimming alongside, with a corner of the dinghy in its mouth. The seal was swimming against the current, trying to take Wayne back to the shore. By now, Wayne's parents had managed to alert the Coastguard, who launched their own boat to rescue him. The seal held the dinghy against the current until they arrived. As soon as Wayne was aboard their boat, the seal seemed to wave – then dived back beneath the waves, its job over now that Wayne was safe.

You hear so many terrible stories about fishermen and dolphins, that it's a pleasure to hear one about the two supposed enemies actually working in partnership! For nearly 150 years, the fishermen of Laguna in Brazil and a school of dolphins have worked together to help each other catch fish! The fishermen wade out into the surf and a dolphin will indicate where the fish are by doing a special kind of roll on top of the water. Fishermen say that they can even tell how many fish there are by the way the dolphins roll over. The dolphins get something out of it too. When the fishermen cast their nets, the schools of fish break up, leaving them easy prey for the dolphins waiting just off the beach.

This isn't a one-off. Thousands of years ago, the ancient Greeks reported dolphins helping fishermen with their catches.

Drugs can be hidden in the smallest places, safely out of the reach even of little sniffer dogs. With that in mind, the Canadian authorities have trained gerbils to sniff out illegal substances. After weeks of intensive training at a secret government research centre, the gerbils are sent into Canadian prisons to seek out the contraband.

Gerbils aren't the only unusual animals employed to find contraband. The police in New Jersey use the very special talents of 'Officer Ferris', a Vietnamese potbellied pig, to sniff out illegal drugs.

Some dogs have proven themselves as much at home in the air as they are on the ground, and during wartime, many pets became air force mascots.

One of the most famous American bombers during the Second World War was the B-17 'Flying Fortress', the Memphis Belle. The aircraft is well documented (it was the subject of two films) but less well known is her mascot, a small terrier called Stuka, a veteran of 25 bombing missions!

Another flying dog was a collie named Lieutenant Shortsnorter Gremlin. She was one of the mascots of the US Army Air Force and had an impressive record for, well, aerial dogfights. Lt Gremlin even had her own logbook and after the war this showed more than 225 hours spent in the air, travelling more than 30,000 miles over occupied Europe.

A dog with more flying hours, however, was a German shepherd called Babe. She flew with the crews of the 6th Air Force Heavy Bombardment Division and clocked up 500 hours in a Flying Fortress. Babe's favourite flights were on bombing runs, where she would crouch next to the cameraman responsible for recording bomb explosions. Her trick was to howl above the noise of the engines to let the photographer know when the bombs had been released.

Skippy was a mongrel pup stationed at a US Air Force base in North Africa and was so popular that he even had a B-17 bomber named after him, complete with his name and picture painted on the nose. Skippy had his own miniature flying helmet and regularly flew on the plane that bore his name.

Lucky, another flying dog, has the distinction of being the first dog to fly a bombing mission over Guam in the Pacific. He joined the crew of a US Army 7th Air Force Liberator. Lucky didn't bother with an oxygen mask for high altitude flights – he preferred to snuggle up in the fuselage and sleep.

Now sharing the cockpit with a canine is one thing, but how many pilots would like to fly alongside a bear? Well, the crew of the 390th Bomb Group did. The bear's name was Cuddles and by all accounts he was as comfortable several thousand feet up, as he was in a tree. Similarly, Gertie, a sloth, travelled with one of the aircrew of the USAAF, gaining notoriety as the first (and probably only) sloth to lead bombing raids over Tokyo.

The aircrews of the 6th Air Force Fighter Squadron were less adventurous. They settled for a racoon called Willie, who accompanied them on duty. Willie was fascinated with looking out of the cockpit windows and soon became known as the 'Flying Coon'.

Sometimes even birds need flying lessons and one of these trainee aviators is Edward, a condor bred in captivity at Chester Zoo. Although he's three, he still can't fly – so falconer Michael Hardy has been called in as one of his flying instructors.

The Hawk Conservancy in Wayhill, Hampshire is the site of these lessons. Here they've built a 30-foot-high hill to recreate the condor's natural mountain habitat. Every day, for hours at a time, Michael and his colleagues run up and down flapping their arms while Edward looks on, slightly mystified at the behaviour of his human trainers.

In the wild, condors are brought up in nests perched high in the Andes. They're normally taught to fly before they're one and the method is quite simple. According to the Conservancy's director, Ashley Smith, they're simply pushed out by their mothers and 'have up to 3,000 feet to learn how to fly before they hit the ground. Edward hasn't had this opportunity, so we are now having to teach him.'

It looks like the training during March and April of 1996 paid off, since Edward can now take off and fly in a straight line. But there's still a lot of work to be done. According to Ashley, 'We're going to keep at it until Edward can soar and circle like other condors do.'

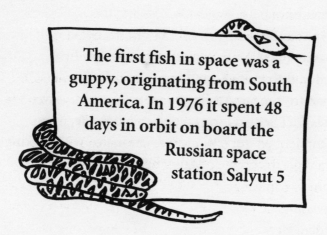

The first fish in space was a guppy, originating from South America. In 1976 it spent 48 days in orbit on board the Russian space station Salyut 5

Jib the canary was one of the widest-travelled birds in the world – but most of the miles he covered were by sea rather than air, on board the SS *Nea Hellas* in 1943–44. Jib joined the ship in Algeria and delighted the crew with his beautiful singing, taking their minds off the war. He would even perform for them in open air concerts on deck. Jib travelled to

Italy, England, South Africa and Burma. In South Africa, he attracted the attention of several cats. The crew bought a duck to keep the cats at bay and it soon proved to be an effective bodyguard for the canary crooner.

Gatwick airport used to be a goat farm

A keen gardener in America used to be accompanied by his devoted golden retriever whenever he went to inspect his vegetables. Every summer evening he and the dog would make their way through the vegetable patch, filling up a large basket with ripe aubergines, peppers and tomatoes before leaving the basket outside the back door of his house.

Then, one day, the man fell ill and was unable to go outside and his son had to come and look after him. As the days went by the vegetable basket lay empty on the porch steps. Then one evening, the son looked out of the window and happened to see the dog in the vegetable garden. He tapped on the window and shouted to him to come in.

The next evening, he looked out and again the dog was in the vegetable garden. He went outside to call the dog in and was surprised to see that the vegetable basket was overflowing with vegetables and fruit. Who could possibly have filled it? He picked up a piece of fruit and then another, noticing that on each one there were four tiny teeth marks in the skin showing where they had been carried out of the vegetable garden before being gently deposited in the basket . . .

Chapter Five

SMARTER THAN THE
AVERAGE BEAR

Forget bungee jumping – the next big thing is *bunny jumping*! Rabbit show-jumping, to give it its proper title. What does it look like? It's just like the Horse of the Year Show – except with rabbits and rather smaller fences. It's already caught on in Sweden, where thousands of people turn out to see rabbit show-jumping events, and top rabbits enjoy the kind of following normally reserved for pop stars! Led around the course on a leash, super-fit bunnies hop against the clock, gracefully leaping over fences two feet high. There's even a water jump. The Harvey Smith of the Swedish rabbit show-jumping world goes by the grand name of *Flames of Fame* and has already won a whole mantelpiece of trophies for his proud owner, Louise Janssen. If your rabbit's not already in training, you'd better get it started now!

It was early morning in the Melander household in a quiet suburb of Little Rock, Arkansas. Twenty-six-year-old Lucille Melander was abruptly woken up by her Russian blue cat Bartholomew, bashing at her nose with his paw. She shouted at him and shook him off her bed – and then smelt smoke. The house was on fire. Lucille jumped out of bed and found a fire raging out of control in her living room. As she raced to grab her eighteen-month-old twin girls from their cots in the nursery, Bartholomew went with her. When Lucille became lost in the thick smoke and took a wrong turning he nipped at her ankles, setting her back on track again for the nursery. She grabbed her daughters and fled outside with the cat at her heels. 'Bartholomew was the one who saved our lives,' she said later. 'He certainly proved his love for me and for my daughters!'

A three-year-old cat with the strange name of Ugly Sister was the heroine of the hour in July 1995 when she saved her owners from almost certain death at their home in Beijing, China. In the middle of the night, Ugly Sister sensed that something was wrong and woke up her owner, Li Shuhua and his family, by frantically miaowing and scratching at their legs. As soon as she saw they were awake, Ugly Sister sprang on to the windowsill and pushed open the window, ready to jump. When her owners didn't try to follow her, she sprang back down from the sill and started clawing at their legs again. It was at this point that Li noticed mud was started to come away from the walls of the two-storey clay house they lived in. He rushed his family outside, Ugly Sister racing around their heels, and seconds later their home collapsed into a heap of rubble.

Commando sheep are at it again down in deepest Hampshire, employing SAS-style tactics to run amok in the quiet little village of Bramshaw. Tired of having their prized lawns and gardens reduced to tatters by hungry sheep, many local residents have installed cattle grids at the ends of their driveways to keep them out. However, they admit they've been outwitted by the sheer ingenuity of the local sheep population. Stunned villagers have reported one sheep throwing itself across the grid to form a bridge – and then letting the other members of the flock trot over his back to get at the lawns and flowerbeds beyond. The local parish council chairman and ex-Marine, Jack Sturgess, recognised the tactic. 'They use the same system the Royal Marines used for crossing barbed wire,' he says. 'One man would cross his arms over his rifle and lie down on the coil, while his colleagues would use him as a bridge. These sheep are a pretty resourceful lot!'

> **It is well documented that a pig's intelligence is more like that of a dolphin than that of any other farmyard animal**

The smartest animal in the world may not be the human being – or the dolphin, for that matter. It could very possibly be the African elephant nose fish. Scientists have recently discovered that this small salt-water fish has a brain that weighs 3.1 per cent of its body mass, which is far more than ours does. Furthermore, thinking accounts for over 60 per cent of all the energy it uses up. What does it think about? No one knows...

Pippen the budgie is Britain's brightest bird. He can speak English, French, Japanese and Afrikaans – and quote Shakespeare. 'He's a fast learner,' says his owner Mrs Charley Fergusson of Clifton, York. 'He really is an entertaining character and I take him wherever I go to keep me company.'

Pippen's command of French includes the phrases '*Je m'appelle Pippen*' (My name is Pippen) and '*Je suis un bon oiseau*' (I'm a good bird). Sadly, however, that's not quite true. Pippen can swear like a sailor in all four of his languages and loves nothing more than to artfully rewrite Shakespeare, coming out with phrases like '*to be or not to be . . . a naughty boy*'. Pippen's greatest collection of swear words is in Afrikaans and he chooses his moments to let fly with them. 'That's what he uses on next-door's cat,' Mrs Fergusson admits.

Scientists are on their way to confirming what we pet lovers have known for years – dogs are psychic! A British research team put hidden cameras in houses with dogs whose owners were at work – and then watched them. An astounding 48 per cent of the dogs being filmed knew when their owner was about to leave work and began to wait by the window for them! The scientists have ruled out conventional explanations, like car engine noise and regular routine, because it made no difference if the owner came back at different times or by a different method of transport. The dogs still knew! Leading this extraordinary research is Dr Rupert Sheldrake, former director of cell biology and biochemistry at Cambridge University. He explains the bond between dog and owner by something called a 'morphic field', a psychic connection just like that which allows flocks of birds to suddenly wheel and turn together as if they all had the same thought at the same time. 'If our intentions can affect animals at a distance, this illustrates that the world view our society is founded on is too limited,' says Dr Sheldrake. 'There is a much stronger connection between humans and nature than we thought.'

Tony Brown-Griffin's collie dog Rupert has an amazing talent. He can tell – up to 45 minutes in advance – if his mistress is going to have an epileptic attack, and warns her of the danger so that she can lie down and prepare herself. Even more amazing, Rupert wasn't specially trained to do this. He was just a common or garden collie Tony rescued from owners who were maltreating him. Since his talent for predicting seizures became known, Rupert has received further special training from Val Strong of Support Dogs. Now Rupert can give different signals for different kinds of epileptic attack, fetch a cordless phone and set off a smoke alarm to alert neighbours if Tony needs help.

More research is now being done into providing trained support dogs for epilepsy sufferers – but researchers first need to know exactly how dogs can sense attacks. At the moment, they think that a scent may be released by chemical changes in the brain, or there may be minute changes in the sufferer's behaviour which humans won't spot – but a dog will. It's vital research because, as Tony herself says, having a dog like Rupert has made all the difference. 'Before I had Rupert to help, I felt trapped in my house. I hardly ever went out. It was simply too dangerous. Rupert has transformed my life!'

Momoko the macaque is a real action monkey. She water-skis, windsurfs and even goes deep-sea diving! Momoko started life as a homeless stray in Nagasaki, Japan. The cheeky monkey was caught stealing fruit from grocers and was going to be put down, until Katsumi Nakajima intervened. He persuaded the authorities to let him adopt Momoko – and now she's his constant companion.

Katsumi is a keen watersports enthusiast and – in a classic case of 'monkey-see, monkey-do' – Momoko started to copy her master. Seeing that Momoko had an interest in watersports, Katsumi started to train her and now she's better at some sports than he is! With her natural sense of balance, Momoko finds windsurfing on her own little board a doddle, and she tackles 30-feet-high ramps with ease when she's water-skiing behind Katsumi's speedboat.

Momoko's favourite pastime is going deep-sea diving with her human pal. Resplendent in her own bright yellow wetsuit and diving helmet, she joins Katsumi on expeditions to explore the sea bed, perching on the underwater coral reefs and watching in wonder as fish swim all around her.

According to experts, Momoko's passion for the water isn't as odd as it seems. Macaque monkeys are good swimmers and have been known to catch fish by diving off tree branches into the water. Momoko, it seems, has just taken her natural talents and made the most of them.

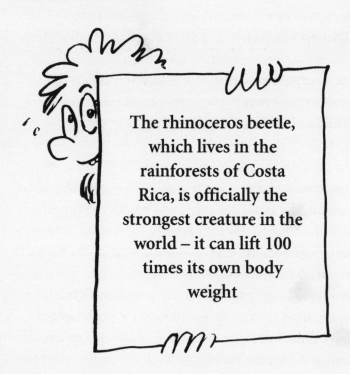

The rhinoceros beetle, which lives in the rainforests of Costa Rica, is officially the strongest creature in the world – it can lift 100 times its own body weight

Performing elephants in circus shows can have a very rough time of it. Mary the elephant is a typical example. She hated performing for the crowds, and her owners considered her stupid, dangerous and bad-tempered, so they sold her.

Luckily for Mary she was bought by the Elephant Sanctuary set up by Scott and Heidi Riddle in California. Now Mary is perfectly happy, and spends her time painting! Working with acrylic paints, she produces canvases which sell for up to $250 each, helping to bring the sanctuary in much-needed cash. Away from the harsh regime of the circus, she's now very friendly and enjoys giving visitors rides on her back.

Masius was an energetic cat who was forever running around, chasing his tail or one of his many toys in the house where he lived with Mr Zagorski.

Mr Zagorski was a keen card player and this particular evening, 12 people were taking part in a bridge tournament in his lounge.

They were so engrossed in their cards that it wasn't until halfway through the evening that someone noticed that Masius wasn't his usual self. He was sitting on a settee, frozen like a statue, staring intently at the ceiling.

At first the guests thought this was funny but after watching him for a few minutes it became unnerving. No one said a word. They all looked at the cat, at the ceiling, and back to the cat again. Then without warning, the peace was shattered. Masius gave a piercing wail and leapt off the sofa, bounding through the kitchen and out of the back door.

Mr Zagorski and his guests rushed out after him. Seconds later there was a loud grating noise followed by an almighty roar. A massive slab of the concrete ceiling above had collapsed on to the lounge, flattening the card tables.

Somehow Masius had known of the impending accident – his sixth sense had saved not only his owner, but 11 of his close friends.

A large earthquake hit the San Francisco Bay area on 17 October 1989 but for a few weeks before the disaster, large numbers of cats had gone missing. Did they know that an earthquake was imminent?

The answer must be 'possibly'. It is thought that cats are sensitive to changes in the earth's magnetic field – or that they may even be able to feel tiny vibrations in the ground before an earthquake actually strikes.

Scientists in the United States and China are studying cat behaviour as a method of helping them predict when an earthquake will hit.

Dogs, too, often act strangely just before a quake. In Tashkent, Uzbekistan, just before a severe earthquake in 1966, a dog chased a Russian woman out of her own house minutes before the tremor destroyed the whole building.

Apart from predicting earthquakes, pets have also been known to predict man-made disasters. During the war, the British battleship HMS *Salmon* had two cats on board who normally led very sedate lives. However, one day, just as they were coming into port, they tried to leave the ship by running down the gangplank – but their way was barred by two sailors on guard. They were more successful at the next opportunity. A tug had tied up alongside and they jumped aboard and went into hiding.

HMS *Salmon* had to leave without them. Later that same day she was torpedoed, and sank with all hands. The ship's cats seem to have had an uncanny premonition of the disaster.

Sterling the poodle displayed an uncanny knack for card tricks when he appeared on the David Letterman show in the USA. Sterling's owner took an ordinary pack of playing cards, shuffled them and got David Letterman to take a card out at random and show it to the camera.

The card was then placed back in the pack, and the pack placed on the studio floor. Sterling the poodle then knocked the cards around, studying them intently, before indicating one of them. Yes, you've guessed it: it was the card originally chosen.

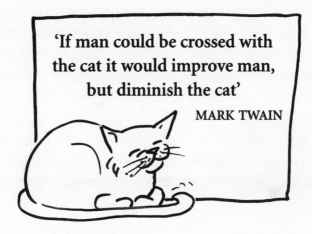

'If man could be crossed with the cat it would improve man, but diminish the cat'

MARK TWAIN

The Viccellio family of Norfolk, Virginia were keen readers and their house was packed with books. Even their golden retriever Wofford seemed to share their love of books and proudly paraded around the house carrying books gently in his teeth. He even slept among piles of books on the floor.

But one day in 1993 his love of books landed him in trouble with the law. It started when he sneaked out through a hole in the fence. Most dogs would make the most of their freedom, maybe checking out the whereabouts of some lady dogs or paying a visit to the butcher's. Not Wofford – he headed straight for the nearby Larchmont Library.

He picked a book up from one of the displays and headed over to the checkout counter. One of the librarians recalled seeing Wofford waiting patiently in the queue with the book in his mouth. He phoned the number on the dog's collar but no one was in. Eventually Mr Viccellio returned home, got the message and immediately rushed to the library to collect Wofford – and a summons to appear in court for not controlling his dog.

Mr Viccellio appeared before the judge and explained that Wofford wasn't trying to steal a book from the library: he was queuing in the checkout line like a good citizen. The judge was amused by this and dropped all charges against Wofford.

This was a relief to his owner. The last thing he wanted was his dog getting the book thrown at him!

Shandy, a Siamese cat owned by Faye Murrell, appeared on the American TV show, *Astonishing Animals*. His trick was in keeping with his origin – scooping up food proficiently with a chopstick attached to one of his paws.

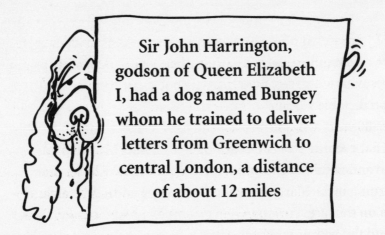

Sir John Harrington, godson of Queen Elizabeth I, had a dog named Bungey whom he trained to deliver letters from Greenwich to central London, a distance of about 12 miles

Zoologists have long been fascinated by animals who develop a particular skill and then communicate it to their fellow creatures. When a blue tit or sparrow learns how to peck holes in the foil tops of milk bottles, the other birds pick up the trick by watching them, but when cows organised a rota among the herd, animal experts could only scratch their heads in puzzlement.

The cows in one field had to leave their young calves behind when they made their way down a steep hill to drink. The calves, who were still being weaned, didn't need any of the water and in any case weren't able to manage the incline. The problem was that when the cows left, wild dogs or foxes would savage their young and many calves died this way.

Then one day, the farmer noticed that instead of all the cows moving off to the river, one stayed behind to protect the young. The next day the same thing happened, but a different cow stayed behind. The following day the rota changed once more. This amazing spectacle continued day after day until all the cows had taken a turn being 'guard cow'.

To this day, no one knows how they organised themselves in this manner.

In late March 1944, Gianni and Irma was living in a small farmhouse just outside the Italian town of San Sebastiano al Vesuvius with Toto, their cat. Living so near to the unpredictable volcano didn't worry them – the last eruption had been 80 years ago, and anyway, they had to get on with their lives.

That evening Toto was particularly restless. He was off his food and wouldn't stay indoors. At about midnight on the morning of 21 March he woke Gianni by painfully scratching him on the face. Furious, Gianni jumped up and chased Toto round the bedroom. But instead of being scared, Toto stood his

ground, hissing and clawing at the air. By this time, Irma had
woken and was surprised to see Toto behaving so strangely. He
was usually such a docile cat – it was as if he was possessed. Irma
believed that Toto was trying to tell them something so, after a
long argument, she persuaded her husband that they should
spend the rest of the night at her sister's house in a different
neighbourhood.

They'd been gone an hour when Vesuvius erupted and a sea of
molten lava gushed from its crater, completely engulfing their
town. The eruption killed 30 people, wiped out the town and
left 5,000 homeless.

Gianni and Irma were grateful for the predictive powers of
Toto. They'd lost their house but he'd saved their lives.

One of the most famous American cats of all time was
Napoleon, who belonged to Mrs Fanny de Shields of
Baltimore in the 1930s.

Napoleon had an uncanny ability to predict the weather
better than any weatherman – which made him very popular
with the local farmers. Even more uncannily, he could predict
the weather in his sleep! It was said that if he snoozed on his
stomach then rain would fall. If he slept on his side, it would
stay dry. His forecasts were so accurate that they were even
published in the local paper. During the severe drought of the
1930s he lay on his side for weeks and weeks. Anxious farmers
who couldn't wait for the paper would pester Fanny every few
hours just to see if Napoleon was sleeping on his stomach yet . . .

Today, in the town of Roseberg in Oregon, local goats are
valued for their skill as weather forecasters. If the herd can be
seen grazing on the summit of Mount Nebo, then the day will be
sunny. If they're near the bottom, it's likely to rain. And if the
graze halfway up it'll be overcast. Records have shown that the

goats are 90 per cent accurate in the weather they predict. In the same period, the local weather service was right just 65 per cent of the time!

A famous circus act in nineteenth-century Italy was Pietro Capelli and his cats. Pietro taught his travelling troupe of cats to play musical instruments, swing from a trapeze and juggle balls with their hind legs. Pietro spoke three languages – and his cats understood commands given in all of them.

> **The North American black woodpecker can eat 1,000 ants in a single feeding, hammering way at trees 15 times a second. To withstand these sort of jolts, the birds' beak and brain have their own built-in 'shock absorbers'**

Pet pigs are far more intelligent than dogs, according to pig-owner Heather Powles, whose two Vietnamese potbellied pigs Roger and Charlie wowed the crowd at the 1996 Pet Pig Show. Heather had trained the porcine pair to sit on command, to work their way through a complicated obstacle course complete with tunnels and bridges, and to blow a Glenn Miller(ish) tune on some horns.

It only took her a day – and a few packets of Ryvita – to teach the pigs to sit. 'Compare that to my dog,' says Heather. 'It took three weeks to get him to offer me his paw . . .'

In America, pigs have already been banned from competing in some obedience contests because they showed up the dogs so badly!

Just how intelligent are pigs? Researchers at Pennsylvania State University are trying to find out – by getting the porkers to play video games. The pigs, Hamlet and Omelette, operate the joystick with their snouts and are rewarded with tasty treats for moving objects about on the screen. 'There's a lot going on in pigs' minds that we haven't really thought of,' says Professor Stanley Curtis of the university. 'Previous research has shown they're pretty darned quick animals! We've done this type of test before on apes, but that was easier because they have hands to operate the joystick.'

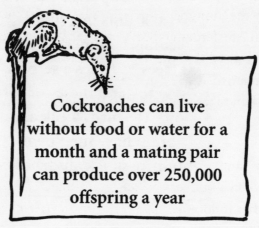

Cockroaches can live without food or water for a month and a mating pair can produce over 250,000 offspring a year

Siva the rescue mongrel came to live with Ted Davenport in Topsham – and soon revealed an exceptional talent as a 'safebreaker'. She got into the fridge and pigged out on cheese, butter and a side of ham. A battle of wills then ensued. Ted tried string, child-proof locks, a superglued clasp and even a thick canvas strap. Siva still worked out how to open the fridge and help herself. In desperation, Ted had to strap the fridge closed and turned it to face the wall!

Toby, the Carlisle station cat, lived in the station buffet, but his first love was travel. The LMS (London, Midland and Scottish) gave the little black cat a special season ticket and a tag around his neck saying 'If found, please return to Carlisle station'. He then set off on his great railway journeys but for some reason would only ever get on a northbound train out of Carlisle, shunning the south. After 50 journeys, the stationmaster gave up logging Toby's travels and just let him get on with it. His longest recorded journey was 245 miles to Aberdeen and his favourite trains to catch a ride on were, not surprisingly, fish trains.

Ricky the mongrel is a regular sight on the number 14 bus in Amsterdam – but he never pays his fare. Somehow, the dog has realised that the bus takes him close to a café owned by a family relative. Ricky hops off the bus, goes in for a fuss and a feed, and then takes a later bus home again!

Mary Tanner of Ware was sitting at home watching the TV when a budgerigar flew in through the open window, perched on her indoor aerial and chirped its telephone number repeatedly. She rang the number the bird gave her and its relieved owners drove over to pick it up later the same day.

A budgerigar which escaped from its home in Nottingham in August 1982 was back within a couple of hours. It was found by a schoolboy who took it round to the address the budgie kept repeating.

The most talented talking bird of all was probably the mynah bird belonging to the British explorer Carveth Wells. Carveth found the bird in a tree while exploring the Malayan jungle and named him Raffles. He was taken back to America where he became a sensation. As well as acquiring a huge vocabulary, Raffles learned how to sing several songs in tune and would sing the 'Star Spangled Banner' at the sight of the flag. He would also play dead on command, and allow himself to be carried around on his owner's head. He earned over $15,000 in one year from radio and stage appearances. Walt Disney was so impressed with Raffles that he threw a party in his honour.

Raffles travelled all over the United States, visiting wounded soldiers who'd returned from overseas. He also helped the war effort by selling war bonds. At bond-selling rallies, Raffles would perform Irving Berlin's popular song, 'You're in the Army Now'. These performances led to the sale of over one million dollars' worth of war bonds.

In honour of his sterling work Raffles was awarded the prestigious Lavender Heart in 1943. (This award is the equivalent to the US Purple Heart Award, but given to animals sustaining injuries.) Raffles lived to see victory, but died the following year aged eight. For about 30 years his mounted body was on display at the Museum of Natural History in New York.

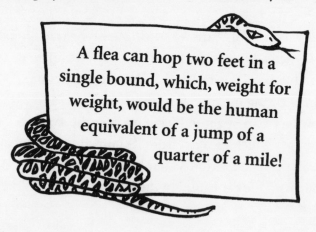

A flea can hop two feet in a single bound, which, weight for weight, would be the human equivalent of a jump of a quarter of a mile!

Chapter Six
CREATURE COMFORTS

A Texas rancher has got round the problem of calling his cows back to the barn for feeding – he's equipped some of them with pagers! These cows have been trained to associate the 'beeping' of the pager with feeding, so that when the rancher wants them to come in for feeding, he just dials their number. The cows with the pagers make for the barn and the others follow . . .

Technology seems to be all the rage with farmers in Texas. Another one has equipped some of his herd with Global Positioning Satellite receivers. From his remote display the farmer can tell the position of cows on his farm to within a few yards.

Sadly, leopards are an increasingly rare species these days, so when Nikita the leopard got pregnant at Basildon Zoo in 1992, there was considerable excitement. However, it turned out that Nikita didn't share her keeper's enthusiasm and she rejected her two tiny cubs – Peanut and Chyna – almost as soon as they were born. Head keeper Michelle Surcouf had to find an answer – and fast! Luckily, her own ginger cat, Velcro, had just had kittens and Michelle introduced the leopard cubs to the litter. Velcro – who got her name because she used to cling on to Michelle's leg as a kitten – immediately accepted the cubs. She nurtured the leopard cubs through the crucial first six weeks of their lives – by which time Peanut and Chyna were getting a bit too big for her to handle – after which they could rejoin their natural mother.

'She's a wonderful cat,' says Michelle. 'She hunts and kills like any other cat, but if I give her small animals to look after she doesn't hurt them.' Peanut and Chyna weren't Velcro's first foster children. Velcro has also adopted and nurtured abandoned baby meerkats, which were no bigger than a mouse.

A gerbil with a mate is a happy gerbil. That's the finding of scientists at Leeds University. They discovered that if a female gerbil is separated from her partner for any length of time, she gets depressed and can't sleep

Most little girls want a puppy or a pony of their very own, but three-year-old Cyanne Nott obviously thinks a little bigger. She has Samantha – a baby white rhino – to love and look after. Cyanne's father Colin is the senior ranger in a game reserve in Zimbabwe and he rescued Samantha after her mother became too old and sickly to feed her. While Samantha was nervous around adult humans, she took an almost immediate liking to little Cyanne and the two are now devoted to each other. The 600lb rhino, who stands about as tall as her human friend, follows her about and is incredibly gentle with her, nuzzling her affectionately and even eating treats out of Cyanne's hand. Cyanne is also helping to feed Samantha properly: at six months the rhino is guzzling down over 60 pints of milk a day!

The Bible talks about 'the lion lying down with the lamb'. It sounds unlikely, but in 1996 it actually happened at Paradise Wildlife Park in Broxbourne, Hertfordshire! Ellis the lamb had been rejected by his mum when just a few hours old and was being raised by staff at the Park. Despite all the human attention, he still seemed lonely. At the same time, Turkana the African black-maned lion cub had been removed from his folks to recover from a hernia operation and was pining for his mother. Staff hit upon the unlikely idea of introducing the lonely lamb and lion cub to each other. Against all expectations they got along like a house on fire, frolicking and playing and generally wearing each other out. The little lion cub showed no signs of aggression towards the lamb, and Ellis showed his affection by nuzzling the cub at every opportunity. Of course, it couldn't last. As Turkana grew, he had to be separated from his friend again, not because he would intentionally have harmed Ellis, but with his sheer strength and power he could have hurt him during play.

While the two were together the lamb helped the lion in another way too. Ellis and his best friend cuddled up and posed together for visitors' cameras to help raise money for *Project LifeLion*, which helps to save Turkana's relatives in Africa's Serengeti.

Angus the bloodhound's favourite possession was a pair of his master's slippers. Ever since he was a pup he had slept with them and whenever he was sad, he'd chew on them for comfort. Eventually they became so tattered and disgusting that his owners, the Harrison family from Pudsey, West Yorkshire, decided to throw them out while Angus was on walkies. Mr Harrison dumped them in a rubbish skip on an industrial estate and thought no more about it.

The next day, Angus was out on walkies when he suddenly bolted off. An hour later he returned – with his beloved burgundy size 9 slippers clutched in his jaws. Like a true bloodhound, he had sniffed them out over a mile away, then crossed a busy dual carriageway, hunted down the skip and retrieved the slippers, following a trail over a day old.

'My wife was absolutely amazed when he returned with the slippers,' says Mr Harrison. 'They obviously mean a lot more to him than we realised.' After his amazing feat, Angus has now been promised that he can keep his beloved slippers.

Multi-millionairess chat show queen, Oprah Winfrey revised her will to ensure that when she dies, her pampered pooch Solomon can continue to have his hair cut. But it's not any old haircut. The chocolate brown cocker spaniel has his coat trimmed once a week at the dog salon at the exclusive Ritz Carlton Hotel in Chicago where each trim costs £150. A snip, if you ask me.

A Russian thief got the shock of his life when he tried to snatch the fur hat off a passer-by's head. The 'hat' was actually a curled up Siamese cat. None too happy about being woken up so roughly, the cat flew at the thief and sank its claws and teeth into his arm. The thief fled. The cat's owner, who lives in the bitterly cold region of north-eastern Russia called Vologda, later explained to reporters that he had decided to wear his cat on his head as a protection against the vicious sub-zero winds blowing that day . . .

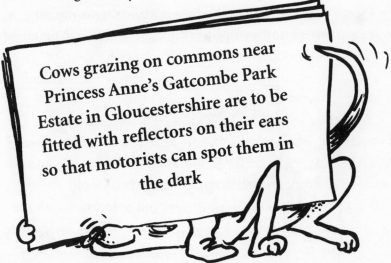

Cows grazing on commons near Princess Anne's Gatcombe Park Estate in Gloucestershire are to be fitted with reflectors on their ears so that motorists can spot them in the dark

The champion fat cat of the world is a chubby fellow by the name of Himmy. A tabby cat owned by Thomas Vyse from Cairns in Queensland, Himmy tipped the scales at a colossal 46lb in 1992 and wears a whopping 33-inch collar. He's so heavy that Thomas has to push him around in a wheelbarrow.

Fancy pampering your pet hound next time he's dog tired? For a mere £9,995 you can buy him an ornate dog bed from the 1996 Harrods Christmas gift catalogue. Made in France, the mahogany four-poster 'pooch palace' comes complete with satin bedding and is crowned with a plume of green ostrich feathers. It's said to be designed after the style of Marie Antoinette's favourite bed.

It's a real 'coup' for the racing pigeons who belong to Warren Coulson of Stanley in County Durham. He's built them a luxury two-storey air-conditioned home worth £7,000. Now, his 40 privileged pigeons get central heating, running water, electric lighting and a balcony with a view!

'Pigeons race best when they're healthy,' Warren explains. 'And you keep them healthy by providing them with airy, warm and dry living conditions.'

The Mexican hairless dog not only whimpers when he's unhappy – he's the only dog in the world to shed tears

Larry Nicolaw's fish and chip shop in the village of Newbold on Avon has succeeded in attracting a very unusual clientele – the ducks from the local river. Larry started off feeding someone's pet duck, and he passed the word on to all the wild ducks that there was free fish and chips going. Soon, mothers would bring their ducklings along and when those babies grew up, they brought along their families in turn. 'I've served quite a few generations now,' says Larry. 'It's a real family business.'

If you feel guilty when you go out to work and leave your dog at home alone, consider this novel solution from America – day care centers for dogs! Angie Weigner has just opened the world's first doggie crèche in Southern Pines, North Carolina.

Called *Pupsi*, the center had piped music – Beethoven, Brahms and, of course, Bach are the favourites – brightly decorated walls with signs saying 'Please no whining', and lots of doggie toys and games. Dogs are walked three times a day and even have stories read to them.

For Angie, who left her job as a highly paid marketing director to open *Pupsi*, it's a dream come true. 'You get to play with dogs all day and people give you money for doing it,' she says.

Cows down on George McCelland's dairy farm in Sonoma County, California, are living in the lap of luxury. George has just spent $25,000 on special rubber mattresses for every one of his 250 cows to lie on at night! They're much happier now, he says, and that means fewer illnesses and more milk.

'The girls lie here content, and some of them are chewing their cud. You can always tell a contented cow when they're chewing their cud,' says George. 'There's an old adage that says the better we take care of them, the better they take care of us.' Along with the new mattresses, George has recently built a new and better barn for his herd and is now looking at other ways to make them even more happy. 'Next, we're thinking of trying pillows for them,' he says.

When it comes to food, dogs in Toledo, Ohio are well catered for. Fido's Fast Food is a drive-through restaurant just for dogs which serves doggie-sized burgers and fries – and provides leftovers in 'people bags'. What I want to know is, who thought of a *drive-through* restaurant for *dogs*?

For reasons best known to themselves, London's Regent's Park Zoo once held an orchestral concert for their animals. It was reported that the crocodiles liked the slow, melancholy tunes but the same music made the rhinos cross. The cheetahs were apparently very bored, but showed some enthusiasm when the orchestra played jazz.

In 1950, Tommy Dorsey and his band performed before monkeys at Philadelphia Zoo. A zoo official described the reaction from the audience as 'negative' . . .

When the pigs at Marwell Zoo near Winchester started to get a little 'riper' than usual, zoo staff knew just what to do. They called in a crack team of aromatherapists to give the pigs a relaxing all-over rub-down with essential oils. After their treatment the pigs apparently not only smelled sweeter but also had considerably sweeter natures.

Imagine six children's pedal cars, wagons and similar toys linked together in a line. Now imagine someone pulling them along. Now imagine (and this is the hardest part) six cats riding in the cars. Well that's how eccentric Ronald McGriff used to take his pet moggies around the streets of New York.

Ant was a pit pony who had worked at the Blaenavon Colliery in Gwent, Wales for 24 years. In that time it's estimated that he travelled 70,000 miles hauling coal trucks through the underground tunnels.

When he retired in 1966 he was bought by an ex-miner, Philip Davies who owned a pub called, appropriately, the Three Horse Shoes. Ant was kept next to the pub in a field which overlooked a bus stop. Soon waiting passengers had something to keep them occupied – they would stroke Ant, feed him treats and generally fuss over him. Numerous people actually missed their bus because they were so engrossed.

From the pub Ant received three *cooked* meals a day, each served with a pint of best stout. He lived out the rest of his days there, and when he died in 1978 he was sadly missed by all the locals, who sent hundreds of cards and flowers in his memory. BBC Wales even announced his death in a news bulletin, and at forty, Ant had held the record for the oldest pit pony in the world.

In England in the eleventh and twelfth centuries it was common for dogs to attend church with their masters. They rested their paws on specially built pews at the back

I've heard of looking at life through rose-coloured spectacles, but this is ridiculous. The Chinese have fitted 140 hens with special, rose-tinted contact lenses. Scientists believe this will make the hens happier and encourage them to lay more eggs – and they say it works on turkeys too!

The chimps at Twycross Zoo have a colour TV in their enclosure. Apparently, they love sports programmes and wildlife documentaries, but more than a few have been caught sitting down to watch *EastEnders* of an evening!

Gorillas at Longleat have satellite TV in their enclosure with a remote control device activated by sound. In this way they can change channels by clapping their hands. I'm not sure how they reacted to *Planet of the Apes* . . .

Egyptian cats were mummified just like humans, with mummified mice sometimes buried with them to provide food for the moggy afterlife!

Every year, the ancient Khmer temple of Lopburi in Thailand holds a special feast for the 200-odd monkeys who hang around the temple grounds. This doesn't just mean putting out a few nuts and bananas. On the contrary, the monks offer up a sumptuous feast. Tables and chairs are set out with best tablecloths. Each monkey is given a napkin and a porcelain drinking glass, then they are allowed to help themselves from heaps of fresh rice, vegetables and dozens of traditional Thai dishes. In a nod to the West, each monkey also gets a can of Coca-Cola. Despite the monks' best efforts, each feast invariably turns into a free-for-all, with the ungrateful monkeys running rampant, upending tables, sitting in the food bowls and squabbling with one another.

And if that's not pampering your pets, then how about the luxury kennels designed by George Papayiannis? He offers Tudor-style kennels complete with a tiled roof and black and white tiled floor – for £4,000. If that's not to your pooch's liking then there's a seven-foot-wide Georgian villa . . .

Architect Metter Farmer is in the same business – providing palaces for pooches. The top of the range Palladian Palace has stone dog statues adorning its turrets, split-level sleeping quarters and a sophisticated air-conditioning system. Miss Farmer produces these luxury kennels in a basic design but owners can have them customised to suit individual dogs' requirements.

If you can't stretch to a luxury home for your pet, you could send them on the holiday of a lifetime! Do you fancy sending your cat to the Fukuoka animal hotel in Japan? It could cost you close to £100 a night, but for that, your pet has a choice of Japanese or international cuisine (including *filet mignon*), a room with leather sofas, panoramic views and Disney cartoons on the telly.

If you've got a dog who's scared of flying or likes to take his holidays closer to home, you might want to consider the Third Bridge Farm Holiday Home for Dogs in Cambridgeshire. Pampered pooches get their own centrally heated room with colour TV and piped music, daily bath and beauty sessions, escorted walkies and 24 hour maid service. Dogs staying over Christmas get a full turkey dinner and a cracker to share with a friend!

There's a Tokyo fashion boutique where you can buy a £5,000 mink coat for your pet or – odder still – a designer bikini. Tokyo also has special doggie slimming clinics where you can put your pooch on a doggy running machine . . .

Mr Shinegori Masuda of Tokyo has a full-time job – teaching yoga to cats. He claims it gives them more self-discipline and helps them to sleep better. The same Mr Masuda also sells a range of special wigs for cats and dogs who have bald patches.

Believe it or not these are all names of real pet products available in the United States: *Wee Wee* pads, *Petrodex* dog toothpaste, *Yuppy Puppy* (treats), *Doggiduds Pet Ponchos*, Cat Condos (bedding) and the *Big Stinky* (litter tray)

A Swiss vet, Dr Ruth Morgenegg, runs her own health farm – for cavies. Alarmed by the number of chubby, lethargic little guinea pigs she was seeing in her surgery, Dr Morgenegg set up a large activity centre in the grounds of her home where cavies can play with pieces of wood, roots and stones, socialise with other guinea pigs or just explore a provocative and stimulating environment. Despite their notorious short-sightedness, cavies love to explore, and the more challenging their environment, the more they enjoy it. While at the 'health farm', the guinea pigs are also put on a strict diet and soon return home slimmer, healthier – and happier.

Meanwhile, Murrayhill Kennels in Leicestershire is the ideal place to take a pooch who's fond of a paddle. They've recently built a large 'therapy pool' in which depressed or out of condition dogs can swim themselves trim again or just kick back and relax. Among the customers are greyhounds and whippets, hoping to improve their performance, and show dogs who want to lose a pound or two before the big event. Human owners can join their pets in the pool if they want to.

Wolf cubs often have the canine equivalent of a 'security blanket' – one treasured little item which they carry everywhere in their mouths. Fox cubs like their 'security blankets' too

In my book *True Animal Tales* I told you about Rastus the motorcycling enthusiast cat, who travels everywhere with his owner Max Corkhill on the handlebars of his vintage 1952 Deluxe Sunbeam motorbike! Rastus even has his own little crash helmet and racing scarf. It's quite a picture. Now, Max and Rastus' good friends, Shirley and David Thomson, have written to me from New Zealand to keep me up to date with their adventures. Apparently Rastus started his biking career in Canada and America and visited many exciting places, like the Grand Canyon, on the handlebars of Max's bike before coming to live in New Zealand. Currently Rastus is a big attraction at fêtes and fairs, like SPCA open days, where he helps to raise a lot of money for charity. In his spare time he likes to hang out with the dogs! That's one tough cat!

Dr Ursula Dietrich, a dentist from San Francisco, has invented the world's first beef-flavoured toothpaste especially for dogs. It's called *Doggydent*

Lincoln-based Perky Pet Foods recently launched the first pet food cans – especially for hedgehogs. The food, called 'Spike's Dinner', is made of chicken and is intended for people who wish to feed hedgehog visitors to their gardens. Animal rescuer Rosemary Sayer, who looks after 80 hedgehogs in her sanctuary in Norfolk, confirmed that her hedgehogs loved it.

Incidentally, contrary to popular belief, if you're lucky enough to have a hedgehog visit your garden you should never give it bread or milk. It's actually dangerous for them. They're carnivores, so cat food or puppy food is a safer bet.

Chapter Seven
BRAVE HEARTS

Bill the cat was devoted to his master. One day, his beloved owner left for work and never returned. He had been badly injured in a railway accident and died in hospital a few days later. All his friends and family turned out for the funeral at the church – and were astonished to find Bill there too. The devoted cat had come to pay his last respects to his master. He walked up to the side of the grave, took a last forlorn look at his master's coffin, and then went home again . . .

Help came from a most unexpected source when Carmarthen farmer Donald Mottram found himself under attack from a prime French Charolais bull. He had driven into the bull's field on a four-wheel quad bike to give a sick calf an injection. He was tending the calf when the bull struck, knocking him and his bike 30 feet across the pasture. As Donald tried to get up, the bull stood over him, kicking him until he lost consciousness. When he came to, he found himself surrounded by his herd of cows. The cows, apparently led by his personal favourite, fourteen-year-old Daisy, had formed a protective circle around him to shield him from the enraged bull. They kept shielding him as he crawled 200 yards to safety, blocking the bull's path every time it attempted to get at Donald.

'They say cows are dumb creatures, but I'm certain my animals knew of the danger I was in and decided to protect me,' says

Donald. 'Some of my favourite cows were in the group – as well as Daisy there was Megan, Amy, Bethan, Mary and Kitty. They undoubtedly saved me from being trampled to death. My cows looked after me so I intend to make sure they have a long and happy life here on the farm. They are now all on extra rations of cow cake.'

When his boat capsized in stormy seas in Nassau Sound in 1983, Jeff Barry found himself floating in the water with sharks closing in. He grabbed two large floating cushions and kicked out for the distant shore. As the first shark moved in, a school of porpoises appeared and swiftly drove the killer away. For more than 12 hours, as Jeff kicked his way through the seas to the shore, every attempt the sharks made to get at him was frustrated by the porpoises. They watched him finally drag himself on to the beach to safety, and then, their job done, they headed out to sea again.

It was routine work for Finnish frontier guard Reijo Savula. As part of an ecological study programme, he and his team were to capture specimens of the local brown bear population, cage them, tag them and then let them go. This time, however, as Reijo tried to secure the poles on the gate of the cage, the brown bear he had captured forced itself free and charged at him, bellowing with anger. A powerful blow from the bear's paw sent him sprawling on to the forest floor, dazed and semi-conscious. In moments, the bear had his powerful jaws clamped around the man's head and was dragging him off into the forest. As his human companions froze in fear or fled, Reijo's faithful mongrel dog Riku came charging to the rescue. He leapt at the bear, sinking his fangs into the bear's flank and refusing to let go as the bear desperately tried to shake him off. Howling with pain, the bear released his grip and turned to attack the dog, allowing Reijo's stunned companions to race in and rescue him. Riku succeeded in driving the bear back into the forest, and then accompanied his master to hospital.

Artie, a Labrador belonging to Lee LeCaptain, loves the water. He can retrieve objects 20 feet down and can hold his breath for nearly three minutes!

Poor Mooch the fire station dog. Although he was the mascot for Fire Engine Company No. 11 in Newark, New Jersey, he was terrified of fire. One wisp of smoke and he'd run for miles. There was no question of taking him out in fire engines on emergency calls. He would panic the moment he saw flames. The firemen jeered at him. Mooch wasn't a proper fireman's dog, they said. Proper firemen's dogs rode the engines with their crew. So Mooch was left to 'mooch' around the fire station while the humans went off to do their duty. He took to wandering the area and soon struck up a friendship with a female dog living in a nearby apartment.

All went well until one day an emergency call came in. A building was ablaze close to the fire station – the building where

Mooch's lady friend lived! The firemen could see the thick black smoke billowing out of the apartment from the fire house. So could Mooch but – rather than giving in to his fear – he raced to the scene and plunged into the burning building. Keeping low under the choking smoke, Mooch sniffed his way to his lady friend, and found her lying unconscious on the floor, overcome by the fumes. He gripped her collar between his teeth and dragged her to safety as the firemen worked to save the burning building.

As you'd expect, Mooch's daring rescue earned him the respect of all the firefighters, who had a medal struck especially for him. For the rest of his life Mooch wore that medal wherever he went – to show the world that he was a true fireman's dog.

When Sergeant Stubby tried to check into a posh New York hotel the reservations clerk refused him admission. You can understand why. After all, he was a dog. He was a Boston terrier-boxer mix to be precise, but what the clerk didn't realise was that Sergeant Stubby was an American war hero.

He saw action in the First World War, serving with distinction alongside the American Army in France with his master, Corporal Conroy. For the wounded soldiers of the war trapped in no man's land, Sergeant Stubby was literally a lifesaver. At great risk – and without being trained for the job – Stubby would scramble out of his trench and head on to the battlefield, weaving around the shell holes and fields of barbed wire in his search for survivors. When he located one, he'd stay beside him, comforting him and barking until he attracted the attention of stretcher bearers. Stubby had enlisted on the Yale University campus, wandering in one day and being adopted by the recruits training there. They smuggled him overseas in 1917 and he saw action in 19 battles, helping to save numerous lives.

He had the uncanny ability of knowing when enemy shells were about to land. As soon as his comrades saw him crouching in the trenches with his paws covering his ears, they too took cover.

On one occasion he joined an infantry charge, barking furiously, and jumped into an enemy foxhole, biting an astonished German soldier on the bottom.

After the war, Stubby became one of the world's first pet therapy dogs, working to cheer up the hundreds of wounded in the field hospitals in France. For his outstanding service, Stubby was promoted to sergeant (outranking his owner!). On his return to America, he was presented to President Woodrow Wilson in a special ceremony where General Pershing personally presented him with a gold medal for valour.

Oh yes, once the desk clerk realised who Stubby was, he was not only allowed in, but was treated like the hero he was.

All cats love to climb, but the champion of them all must be an unnamed four-month-old kitten who conquered the Matterhorn, climbing the summit, 14,688 feet up – and all because he didn't want to be left behind when a group of climbers began their ascent.

It happened on 6 September 1950 and according to *The Times*, the little kitten lived at the Hotel Belvedere, the traditional starting point for climbers attempting the ascent. As one group left, the kitten ran out of the hotel to follow, literally in their footsteps. The paper reports: 'He was soon left behind but after a long and lonely climb reached the Solway Hut (12,556 feet). The next day he climbed still higher.'

The next morning, the little kitten was seen by another group of climbers. He was black and white, so stood out against the snow. They passed him and were convinced that despite his natural climbing skill, he wouldn't get much further and would return back down. They were wrong and again, according to reports, 'Hours later, the cat, miaowing and tail up, reached the summit, where the incredulous climbing party rewarded him with a share of their meal.'

The guide of that party brought the kitten down in his rucksack because, he said, 'Cats climb up much more easily than they climb down!'

'To his dog, every man is Napoleon – hence the popularity of dogs!'
ALDOUS HUXLEY

David Bruce and his wife Pauline of Hayward, California, were strolling to church one crisp winter's day, pushing their two-year-old son, David Junior, along in his buggy. They turned a corner and walking ahead of them was a stray dog which the young David immediately took a liking to.

After much screaming and shouting, David Jr convinced his parents to let him out of the buggy so he could pet the dog. It was a mongrel, but it seemed friendly enough. To their horror, however, little David dashed between two parked cars and into the road, straight into the path of a speeding car. Powerless to move, all Pauline could do was scream in terror. The next thing they knew, the stray dog had darted into the road, turned and knocked little David back towards the kerb and out of danger.

Stunned by what had happened, the child just sat on the kerb bewildered, with the dog standing over him.

Pauline and David Senior couldn't believe their good fortune – their son's life had been saved by the reflexes of an abandoned Rottweiler-spaniel mix. They really wanted to adopt her, but this was impracticable because they lived in an apartment. However, they alerted the local newspaper and it started a campaign to find her a new home. The paper was inundated with offers for the brave dog – now named 'Minnie the Mutt'.

An injured war veteran returning home was a common sight at the height of the Vietnam War, but the wounded, battle-scarred hero being officially welcomed back at a Texan Air Force base in July 1967 was different – he was five years old, and a German shepherd dog.

His name was Nemo, and he was probably amongst the most famous of the sentry dogs used in Vietnam to search for Vietcong guerrillas. Soldiers called these dogs 'guided muzzles' and Nemo was one of the best.

After training at Lackland Air Force base in Texas, Nemo joined the 377th Air Police station at Tan Son Nhut airbase. Here he'd patrol the perimeter fence with his handler, Robert Thorneburg, looking for any Vietcong trying to infiltrate the base.

On a night in December 1966 they were patrolling an area about a quarter of a mile away from the airbase's runways. It was a clear night and the two stood dead still, staring into the distance. Just then, Nemo's ears pricked up and his head cocked to one side. Thorneburg was about to radio for back-up when a sniper's bullet hit him in the arm. A second followed which hit Nemo in the face.

The shots had been fired by four Vietcong guerrillas now clustered around the security fence, trying to cut their way in.

Although badly wounded, Nemo launched himself at the Vietcong, giving his handler the time he needed to radio for help. In seconds, US soldiers arrived on the scene, chasing off the Vietcong. Both handler and dog were then rushed to the base hospital.

Nemo had an emergency tracheotomy and skin grafts and although he was patched up, he lost his right eye. He was soon back on perimeter duty, but was then sent home to Lackland where he could receive better medical care.

Nemo spent his retirement at the base with his own special kennel, complete with a plaque commemorating his heroic action in defending the airbase. This now serves as a permanent reminder of just what a vital role he – and other courageous dogs like him – played in the war effort.

A rogue elephant on the rampage can be a fearful sight and that's exactly what met the gaze of Major Daly as he supervised a pack of elephants unloading grain and rice from a ship at Cawnpore, India, in the hot summer of 1937.

The unloading had been routine until the air was shattered by the blast of a lone bull elephant. With its trunk and sharp tusks raised in defiance it broke out of line and crushed its keeper, before turning on Major Daly's children, who had been watching their father at work. The children froze with fear. There was no escape as four tons of berserk elephant thundered towards them.

The Major and other soldiers were too far away to do anything, but suddenly another cry went up from an ancient bull elephant – Old Soup, said to be nearly 100 years old.

Regardless of his own safety, Old Soup ran towards the rogue creature who was now just yards from the petrified youngsters. Summoning every last reserve of energy, Old Soup hurled himself at his opponent. The two powerful pachyderms collided with an almighty crash just feet from the children, who could only look on in horror.

The ground trembled and dust filled the air as the mighty beasts locked tusks in a fight to the death. The rogue elephant was younger and stronger but Old Soup was more determined. The battle royal seemed to last for ever. Despite being gored again and again, having an ear severed and one of his tusks shattered, Old Soup never gave up. Drawing on his last breath, he charged and, twisting his head at the last moment, managed to sink his one good tusk in the rogue's underbelly, inflicting a mortal wound before collapsing himself.

As the dust settled the Major ran to his children, who were shaken but otherwise unharmed. Old Soup was given medical attention on the spot and soon made a full recovery.

He was retired from the military and went to live with Major Daly – the best bodyguard for his children that he could ever wish for!

A chameleon's tongue can stretch out to twice the length of its body

Greek and Roman literature is rich with tales of dolphins saving the lives of swimmers caught in strong currents, or chased by large predators, but a more recent and substantiated story comes from a Florida woman who was saved from both perils – a deadly undertow and an even deadlier shark.

It was a beautiful warm day and the woman was swimming well within sight of the Florida shoreline when she suddenly got into difficulties with the undertow. In seconds she had been drawn down, water filling her mouth and lungs, before she was thrown up again, gasping for air. This happened three times and each time the swimmer found herself being drawn into deeper and deeper water.

She was totally unaware of the fact that a shark was closing in on her. At this point a lone dolphin bore down on the shark with great speed, aiming its pointed snout at the shark's gills – the only place where an attack would have any effect. Caught totally off guard by the impact, the shark was stunned and its instinct drove it to swim to safety in far deeper waters. The dolphin then turned towards the helpless swimmer, surfaced beneath her, and carried her on its back towards the beach. Near the beach it twisted, shaking the swimmer off, and then pushed her forward on to the sands into the waiting arms of rescuers.

When a mother shrew goes out for a walk with her offspring, they form a chain, each baby shrew clinging hold of the tail of the shrew in front. Zoologists call this 'caravanning'.

One hundred goats owe their lives to one brave dog, a 20-month-old collie called Buddy. He belonged to Matthew Crinkley and lived on a dairy farm at Budd Lake in New Jersey. One morning in 1964 Matthew was awakened by Buddy barking loudly outside his bedroom window. He got up to see smoke and flames pouring out of one of the barns – but what was more astonishing was the sight of Buddy herding goat after goat from the barn to safety, pushing and nudging them out of the way of burning timbers.

Despite suffering burns to his paws, Buddy managed to save all 70 goats, most of who were pregnant. He was also indirectly responsible for saving 30 goats from the neighbouring barn. Matthew had now been alerted to the fire, and was able to soak the roof of that barn to prevent it catching alight as well.

Buddy became the Ken-L Ration Dog Hero of the Year for 1964. After the award ceremony one of their spokesmen said, 'The 100 goats, together with those since born of the expectant mothers, later constituted a flock of nearly 300 goats that would have surely been lost had it not been for this intelligent and devoted collie.'

You wouldn't expect a 10-stone dog to be 'faster than a speeding bullet' but that's exactly what the Fawcett family felt about their Akita dog, Nago.

In 1992 Mrs Fawcett and her three daughters were waiting for the school bus in the town of St Mary, Ontario. Six-year-old Alaina Fawcett was standing apart from her sisters and didn't see the truck that was heading towards her skid on a patch of ice and career out of control. Her mother was frozen to the spot, unable even to scream out, when Nago leapt into action.

The 145lb dog jumped straight into the path of the truck, pushing Alaina into a ditch to safety, a split second before the truck skidded past them.

Miraculously, both Alaina and Nago sustained only a few bruises. For his selfless act of bravery, Nago was welcomed into the Ralston Purina's Animal Hall of Fame in Canada.

Judy the pointer had some incredible adventures and narrow scrapes during the Second World War. Called up for service as HMS *Grasshopper*'s official ship's mascot, in February 1942 she was marooned on a tropical island when her ship was bombed and sunk by Japanese aircraft. Almost immediately she made herself a heroine of the first order by finding a hidden source of fresh water for her surviving crew mates. When the sailors left the island on board a stolen junk, Judy went with them, but they were intercepted by the Japanese and taken to a POW camp. Here, Judy made friends with Leading Aircraftsman Frank Williams. He gave her half his food each day and they soon became the best of friends. To Frank and the other Allied prisoners, Judy was a godsend, keeping their spirits high by fussing over them and barking at her Japanese captors. The Japanese commander felt she was a threat to his authority and ordered her to be destroyed. Somehow, the Allied prisoners thwarted his plan by having Judy officially recognised as a prisoner of war. Furious, the camp commandant then ordered all the prisoners to a camp in Sumatra. Judy, he said, was to stay behind. Once again the prisoners outwitted him, smuggling Judy along with them hidden in a rice sack!

Then disaster struck. The ship carrying Frank and Judy was sunk by an Allied submarine and the two were pulled out of the water by the Japanese and returned to their original POW camp. The commandant couldn't believe it. The damn dog was back again! One of his first orders was for the prisoners to kill – and eat – the dog. However, Judy was whisked into hiding and was liberated along with the camp soon afterwards.

On her return to England, Judy was awarded the Dickin Medal for her amazing bravery, while Frank Williams received the PDSA White Cross of St Giles for his devotion to the dog. Judy lived out the rest of her days with Frank on a farm in Tanzania.

Although Madge Comerford was well into her eighties, she exercised regularly by going on long walks with Venus, her little Jack Russell. On one such occasion in 1972, the pair were taking a leisurely stroll through a field near their home in Sussex. Madge walked on ahead while Venus was scampering around some way behind. Due to failing eyesight, Madge mistook a bull in the field for a cow, and in seconds it had charged her, hitting her squarely and throwing the frail old lady to the ground. While she lay there helpless, the bull tried to gore her. The sound of her screams brought Venus running. The little dog leapt up at the bull and bit it on the nose before being shaken off. Picking herself up, Venus then snapped at the bull's legs until she'd managed to chase it away, giving Madge precious time to recover and pull herself to safety. Venus was unharmed and thanks to the dog's quick action, Madge sustained nothing worse than bruising and a cracked rib.

A male sea otter can weigh almost as much as a German shepherd dog!

The new Polish war memorial in Stamford, Lincolnshire was dedicated in style. While the Polish ambassador and defence attachés paid their respects, a Spitfire, Hurricane and a Lancaster bomber from the Battle of Britain flew in tribute above. The RAF Red Devils' parachute display team performed a jump to salute a fellow paratrooper. A paratrooper called Smokey the sheepdog.

Smokey had been found as a three-month-old pup, cowering in a bombed out building in London. The Polish paratroopers who rescued him brought him back with them to their base in Stamford and he quickly became the camp favourite. Smokey had time for everyone. He played football with the paratroopers by bashing the ball with his nose, and raced alongside them as they trained on the assault course. He even won his own Polish 'Grey Beret' by making two training jumps with his friends, attached to a miniature parachute.

'Smokey was loyal, committed and in every respect a genuine paratrooper,' remembers Dr Wladyslaw Mozdzierz, the man who rescued him. 'He wore our eagle emblem with pride and had his own small parachute. He was always very loving and cheerful – the most faithful friend you could have.'

But then Smokey's mood abruptly changed. His friends were getting ready to parachute into Arnhem and somehow, he seemed to know that many would not be coming back. As preparations for the jump continued, Smokey just pined away and died in the arms of Captain Mozdzierz. A vet who examined Smokey said that he had died from a broken heart. Tragically, Smokey's premonition came true. Dozens of the men he loved so much never returned from the battle of Arnhem, which saw some of the bitterest fighting of the Second World War. Captain Mozdzierz himself won the Polish VC for his gallantry during the battle, but nothing could replace the dog he had lost.

In May 1997, Dr Mozdzierz and four other veterans from the Polish Medical Parachute Company returned to Stamford to be part of the unprecedented ceremony at Smokey's grave, and to pay their last respects to the dog who loved them so much.

A man and a dog, who both left home unannounced and who had never met before, suddenly found themselves drawn together by a bizarre coincidence. It happened in 1984 when a white Samoyed named Laska escaped from her home in the Pennines after a decorator left the front door open. By the time her owner realised she was missing, Laska was long gone.

Meanwhile, Norman Stephenson had left his house about six miles away without telling his wife. He'd gone for a stroll but the weather turned bad and he was soon caught in a heavy storm which made the hilly path he was following very slippery and treacherous. Norman pressed on, hoping the weather would clear up but he slipped and rolled down an embankment into a ditch. Badly hurt, he was unable to move but was still conscious.

Just at this time, Laska was on the same hillside and saw Norman fall. She ran to him and instinctively covered him with her thick fur, protecting him from the bitingly cold wind and rain for over 16 hours. Both Norman and Laska were found the next morning by passing hikers. Norman was taken to hospital and Laska was reunited with her worried owner, none the worse for her ordeal. Was it all just a coincidence or did Laska have some premonition that Norman would be involved in an accident and that she was to save him?

The area where a sixth sense for danger is most needed is in mine detection. It takes a very special dog indeed to become a successful part of a minesweeping team. Dogs are trained to sniff out mines and sit down as soon as they find something. One of the best and bravest mine detection dogs of all was Rickie, a small Welsh sheepdog. Rickie served in France, Holland and Belgium. He was part of a team trying to clear a section of canal embankment in Holland when one of the mines he had already detected, exploded without warning, killing the battalion commander. Despite being wounded by flying shrapnel, Rickie continued his task without hesitation, winning a Dickin Medal in the process.

John Eichelberger's poodle Duke had his ups and downs – but rather more ups and downs than most. He lived at Lakemont Amusement Park in Atloona, Pennsylvania and every day without fail, come rain of shine, he insisted on going for a ride on the Skyliner – a roller coaster that reached up to 65mph. Duke loved the feel of the wind rushing through his fur and, to bring more variety to his life, he soon added other rides to his repertoire, including the equally sensational Octopus and the Tilt-a-Whirl.

John was the park's maintenance director, and had introduced Duke to the rides when he was a puppy. Duke soon got hooked on them and would even join the merry-go-round on his own, or sneak into the queue for the Big Wheel, hoping someone would befriend him and carry him on.

Duke's day began with a swim in the park's lake. He'd then dry himself out during the ride on the Skyliner, which was tested every day before the park opened. If it was really warm, he'd cool off by going down the water slide on his belly.

Duke died in 1993 but in his time at the park he made friends with thousands of children and adults. He's gone now, but the regular visitors still talk fondly about his exploits – Duke the daredevil dog.

Tang was a Newfoundland dog on board the coaster Ethie. As the boat sailed along the coast of Nova Scotia one night in 1919, a storm took hold and dashed her hull against the rocks. Huge waves swept all the lifeboats off the decks and also prevented rescuers on the shore from getting close. The only way the 92 crew and passengers could get to safety was by attaching a lifeline from the *Ethie* to the shore. One man, the best swimmer on board, drowned in the attempt, but Tang jumped in, holding another lifeline in his mouth, and strongly and fearlessly swam against the waves to the waiting rescuers.

This line was attached to a hawser which pulled the ship into safer waters. The crew and passengers, including a baby, were put in a mail bag and then winched to safety.

Lloyd's Insurance of London later presented Tang with a medal in honour of his courage, and this medal was worn with pride on his collar for the rest of his life.

Surely no dog had a more eventful life than Antis the Alsatian. He was discovered as a tiny cowering puppy in a bombed-out German farmhouse during the Second World War by a Czech air gunner called Jan Bozdech. Jan was on the run after his bomber had been shot down and German patrols were out looking for him but, rather than leave the puppy to starve, Jan picked him up and carried him along. They crossed the border together into Nazi-occupied France and headed south, away from the Germans. Antis grew and grew and was soon able to walk beside Jan for some of the way.

They reached the French Mediterranean coast without being caught and decided to head for neutral Algiers, but their stolen plane was shot down over the sea. Both Jan and Antis survived the crash-landing, only to be captured by an Italian convoy and declared prisoners of war.

Their luck still held good, though. A British warship sighted the convoy and shelled it, sinking the ship they were on. Once again they survived and eventually landed in England where Jan joined the RAF.

After so long on the road together, it's hardly surprising that the Alsatian refused to be separated from Jan, even smuggling himself on board Jan's bomber several times. Once there, he'd lie at his master's feet in the bottom of the gun turret and stay there for the duration of the flight.

Only one in every three members of RAF Bomber Command survived the war, but again Jan and Antis beat the odds. At war's end, Jan took Antis back to his native Czechoslovakia with him and man and dog were all ready to settle into a well-earned retirement.

Then Jan fell foul of the Communist authorities and man and dog were suddenly on the road again, fleeing for their lives just as they had done at the start of the war. Antis helped to warn Jan whenever Communist patrols were near and the two made it to the border. Here, their luck ran out. At the border a guard spotted them and raised his gun. Antis leapt at him, knocking him down and standing on his chest, snarling into the terrified soldier's face while Jan dashed the last few yards to safety. Turning back, he called to Antis who leapt off the guard and raced across the border to rejoin Jan.

Jan and Antis finally ended their epic journey in London where, in 1949, Lord Wavell presented Antis with the Dickin Medal.

Most holiday romances are the same. You fall in love for two weeks, worry about how you'll survive on your own when you get back home, but then, a week after arriving back at Gatwick Airport it's all forgotten. Well, Lesley Dean had a holiday romance on the sunny Greek island of Zante with a difference – it involved a ginger tomcat.

The cat in question used to spend the long, hot days curled up next to Lesley on her sun lounger on the beach. She called him Parker for the duration of the holiday. He was always there at the same spot to greet her every morning and they struck up quite a friendship. But what saddened Lesley more than leaving him on Zante was her hotel manager telling her that stray cats are put down after the tourist season. She couldn't help thinking of what would become of poor Parker.

When she got back home to Ash, in Surrey, in fact she became so concerned about his well-being that there was only one thing to do – she had to go back for him.

Luckily, Lesley's husband Peter was an understanding sort of chap and he immediately set out to rescue Parker before the culling began. The journey involved a 1,500-mile flight to Athens followed by a 250-mile bus ride to the coast, a 90-minute ferry ride to the island and a taxi to the beach.

There, Peter managed to find the cat, telling reporters, 'Parker came up to me straight away and I simply put him into a cat basket and set off back home again.' Peter took the same route back, which meant the whole rescue mission was quite costly. The fares amounted to £650, while quarantine fees were a further £2,500. Parker came back to England two days before he would have been killed and when Lesley saw him again, she knew it had been worth every penny. She even made the 32-mile round trip to the cattery where he was being kept, every day, for the whole of his quarantine period.

Although tigers are 100 per cent cat they love to cool down by going swimming!

When Fizo, a young terrier, saw a five-foot-long venomous brown snake sneaking up on a little girl playing in the back garden of her home in Brisbane, Australia, he didn't hesitate. He leapt on to the snake and gripped it in his teeth as the girl ran for safety. Again and again the deadly snake struck, but Fizo refused to let go until the snake was dead. He then collapsed and sank into a coma. His owners rushed him to a clinic, where he was pumped full of an antidote to the venom. He came round several hours later to be hailed as a hero, and the Australian RSPCA awarded him a Purple Heart medal for his bravery!

A dog owner in Vienna trained his terrier to walk down the street with a coin in his mouth, walk into the tobacconist's and then return with a small packet of tobacco.

The dog did this most days for his master and was a familiar sight in the neighbourhood.

A few years later the man moved to Prague and once he'd settled in, he introduced his dog to the local tobacconist and explained what he used to do in Vienna.

The next day, he put a coin in the dog's mouth. The terrier seemed to understand what to do and trotted off down the road with his tail wagging.

That was the last the man saw of his dog that day. He checked, and found that the dog had never reached the tobacconist. After two further days the owner was resigned to the fact that his dog had either got lost or been kidnapped.

On the fourth day, however, the small terrier returned. He was weak and thin, and collapsed on the front step. In his mouth was the packet of tobacco – wrapped in a bag with the address of the old tobacconist in Vienna! The terrier had travelled 120 miles just to carry out his errand.

The Maid's Head pub in Mildenhall, Suffolk, should have been one of the most burglar-proof places around. After all, it had a nine-stone Rottweiler named Sadie guarding it – and Sadie had been fired from her previous job in a security company for being too aggressive. But when burglars broke in early in 1997, Sadie slept right through the event and it was left to little Dougal the toy poodle to save the day. Dougal, who's only 12 inches tall and weighs less than 10lbs, heard the intruders and sprang into action, scaring them so badly they leapt out of a window to escape him!

'Dougal might be a tiny dog but he has the heart of a lion,' says his proud owner Sheila McDonald. 'When he heard the burglars he was really growling and sounding aggressive. He leapt off our bed in one movement and was out of our bedroom door like a shot. He showed no fear and rushed straight downstairs to confront them.'

By the time Mrs McDonald and her husband Tom got downstairs the burglars had gone – and Sadie the Rottweiler was still fast asleep in her basket, gently snoring.

William Milburn was a bird lover who lived in Jarrow, near Durham. He had always fed wild birds and in the last few years of his life one bird in particular, a small, tame song thrush, would swoop down and land on William's head if he was outside, warbling away melodically as William went about his business.

William developed a severe case of flu and died one morning. That day, and for the next two days while the coffin was still in the house, the thrush didn't sing. Then, on the third day, when the pall bearers arrived to carry the coffin out of the house, the thrush burst into a song as beautiful as anything she'd ever sung. She followed the funeral procession as it left for the church but flew away before it reached the cemetery.

Kathie Vaughn was a victim of multiple sclerosis and paralysed from the waist down but that didn't stop her leading a full and active life. She ran her own antiques business where she lived in Indianapolis, Indiana and drove a specially adapted truck.

One day in 1992 she was en route to an antiques fair in Atlanta, Georgia. Beside her in the truck's cab was her faithful Rottweiler, Eve and behind her was a trailer load of antique furniture.

Kathie planned to drive through the night to reach Atlanta but about an hour into her journey the engine gave a loud bang and the truck and trailer swerved off the road. Luckily Kathie managed to control the skid and the truck came to rest on the hard shoulder. Thick smoke was now starting to billow into the cab as the engine caught fire.

Kathie opened the passenger door and Eve jumped down to safety. The smoke was getting thicker, despite the door being open, but it was too late for Kathie to drop down. She had to use her wheelchair to get out of the truck but this was stored in sections next to her. Kathie frantically tried to assemble it but the smoke made her eyes sting – and threatened to suffocate her.

All the time Eve was jumping up, yelping and barking, trying to save her mistress. Eventually she grabbed Kathie's leg where she had no feeling, and dragged her slowly out of the cab and on to the roadside, trying to get her as far away as possible. Eve and Kathie were only twenty feet away when the truck's fuel tanks exploded – but far enough away not to suffer injury. Police and the fire brigade were soon on the scene to take Kathie to hospital and put out the blaze.

Although her antiques were destroyed Kathie recovered from her ordeal. Eve was awarded the American Humane Association's Award for Bravery. A spokesman said it usually took three months to process a nomination and verify its acceptance, but in Eve's case there was no doubt about her heroism. She got the award in less than two weeks.

In 1973 a golden Labrador guide dog called Sally bravely sacrificed her life in order to save her eighty-year-old owner, Bill Chamberlain. A car had mounted the pavement and was heading towards them when Sally pushed Bill out of the way, taking the full impact of the car herself.

Alfons Koller was the trainer of Indra, an Indian elephant owned by a German circus. Well, he was until he was sentenced to a year in prison for drunk driving. He was no sooner locked up than it became obvious that Indra was pining for him.

She looked morose and refused to eat. In a short time, she'd lost 30 stone – and was in a critical condition. After many consultations between the circus owners, animal welfare organisations and the authorities, the court agreed that Alfons could spend the day with Indra but would have to return to prison each night.

This arrangement did the trick and very soon Indra was the same, happy, healthy elephant the circus had known.

Two fully grown brown bears fled in terror when an intruder clambered into their enclosure at London Zoo – and flashed them! A traumatised Rusty (eight years old and male) and a quivering Tumble (nine years old and female) rushed into their keeper's arms for safety and hugged him tight until police arrived to arrest the man.

Chapter Eight
ANIMAL VIPs

Osceola the bald eagle was pining for the sky. He'd lost his right wing after being shot by a hunter and was being nursed back to health in a Tennessee zoo, but his spirits were low. John Stokes, his carer, tried everything he could think of but Osceola kept pining. Then John hit on a novel idea: he'd go hang-gliding and take the injured eagle up with him! There was just one problem – John didn't have the first idea about how to hang-glide. This didn't deter him though. For Osceola's sake he took lessons and then, with the eagle securely harnessed above him, launched himself from a nearby mountain!

'I wanted him to go back into the element he was born to command,' says John. 'I sensed a change in him when we were up there. When we flew near two hawks, he looked at them as though they were the intruders in his kingdom. When they swooped, we swooped. I finally felt I was giving him something back.'

And where there's a hang-gliding bird, can a hang-gliding cat be very far behind? No. Putty Tat the ginger tom loves to go hang-gliding with his mistress Patty Butler. Putty Tat has his own special harness, which straps him securely to Patty every time she leaps off the cliffs near her home in Monterey, California.

The inspiration for the famous poem 'The Owl and the Pussycat' was Foss the cat, who belonged to Edward Lear. The famous writer was so devoted to Foss that when he decided to move, he had his new house built to exactly the same specifications as his old one – just so Foss would feel at home!

Another writer, Jerome K. Jerome, had a very maternal cat who raised a puppy – and a squirrel. Jerome recalls how the puppy grew up thinking it was a cat and tried to miaow and wash its face with its paws! On the other hand, the mother cat was completely confused by the young squirrel. She just couldn't understand why its big bushy tail kept on sticking up in the air, when she repeatedly licked it and pinned it down so that it would look like a normal kitten's tail.

Lucky cow! Emily the heifer was destined for the slaughterhouse but is now an object of worship and may even star in her own Hollywood epic! It all started in November 1995 when Emily was herded into the Arena Slaughterhouse in Hopkinton, Massachusetts. Rather than accepting her fate, she leapt a six-foot-high barrier and bolted for nearby woods, disappearing before she could be recaptured.

The story of Emily's great escape appeared in the local press and touched the hearts of the Randa family. They asked the slaughterhouse if they could keep Emily if they found her, and the slaughterhouse agreed. For 40 days, Meg Randa and her family searched the woods. There were reports that Emily had been running with a herd of wild deer, and learning to live off the land with them. Finally, on Christmas Eve, the Randa family came upon her grazing in a small clearing. 'I made eye contact with her and right away I knew she and I had a special connection,' Meg recalls. Emily returned with them to live on the family farm – but the story doesn't end there. The local Hindu community became convinced that Emily was a messenger from the gods. Her escape was truly miraculous, the date of her escape was religiously significant – and she had markings on her forehead which bore an uncanny resemblance to a map of India.

Now, devout Hindus come from far and wide to see the sacred cow, and to bring Emily delicious treats to feast on. Priests have travelled from as far away as Cambodia to pay their respects and a statue of Gandhi has been erected in the farmyard. Emily still lives with the Randa family, and the rights to her life story have been bought by a Hollywood producer. She has even acted as a bridesmaid at the wedding of one of Meg's friends, enjoying the ceremony immensely, according to Meg.

Meg Randa, while not entirely convinced of Emily's divinity, does believe that we have something to learn from her. 'Ultimately,' she says, 'the message that Emily has to teach us is that animals are thinking, feeling creatures.'

Florence Nightingale owned 60 cats! It was quite common for her to share her bed with five or six of her Persians

Election news just in – Rocky the Racoon has lost his bid to replace the human port commissioner in Port Orford, Oregon – but it was a close-fought contest. Rocky lost by 301 votes to 345 and might have won if his candidature had been announced sooner. The political power machine behind Rocky, the Committee to Elect Rocky Racoon, decided to enter him after hearing unpleasant rumours about the fate of wild animals who dared venture on to the port commissioner's prized strawberry patch. To bring this to the public's attention, Rocky stood on a platform of 'respect for all beings', 'a kinder, gentler community' and 'free strawberries for all'.

After his narrow electoral defeat, Rocky is now said to be taking time out to 'reconsider his options and to forage for nuts and berries'. He hasn't ruled out another attempt at the top . . .

For 20 years, Beerbohm the tabby cat was the unofficial star of the show at London's Globe Theatre. Officially employed as a mascot and mouser, Beerbohm got a taste of the acting bug instead, and would often wander onstage during a

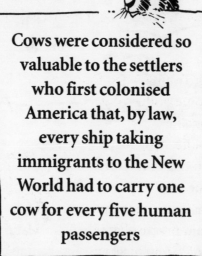

Cows were considered so valuable to the settlers who first colonised America that, by law, every ship taking immigrants to the New World had to carry one cow for every five human passengers

performance. He probably thought himself a great actor – his unscripted entrances always got a huge laugh and a round of applause from the audience!

Beerbohm also shamed himself during the classic production of *The House of Bernard Alba*, which required the stage to be covered with several tons of sand. Unfortunately, Beerbohm mistakenly thought this was the world's largest litter tray and, that night, proceeded to treat it as such.

When he wasn't starring on stage, Beerbohm could often be found wooing Fleur, the Lyric Theatre's cat, and the two were recognised as one of the great couples of the London theatre world!

The first film star cat was a grey stray called Pepper. She just turned up at the studios, wandered on to a set where a comedy scene was being filmed and the script was hastily rewritten to include her! She went on to star with Charlie Chaplin and the Keystone Cops, but her favourite co-star was a Great Dane named Teddy. When Teddy died, Pepper refused to work alongside other canine stars of the era and turned her back on Hollywood for good, preferring to return to her life as a stray.

Author Mark Twain owned four cats which had some of the most exotic names imaginable – Beelzebub, Blatherskite, Apollinaris and Zoroaster – and two that didn't: Buffalo Bill and Sour Mash.

He explained that he named the four so that children could practise 'large and difficult styles of pronunciation'.

The luxury liner *Virginia* was a hive of activity. Prince Rahula had booked a first-class stateroom on board for a five-day voyage to Panama. In preparation for their royal visitor, the ship's crew frantically scrubbed everything on board until it was gleaming. The engines were given a fresh tuning up. The larder was stocked with the finest delicacies and red carpets were laid down from the gangplank to his cabin. Then the officers and ships stewards lined up on the jetty in their best white dress uniforms to greet the prince. A stately car pulled up and the assembled crew got their first sight of Prince Rahula – a very spoiled pet cat with some very rich and indulgent owners!

Cats have also inspired musicians. Apart from the obvious 'Kitten on the Keys' by jazz composer Zez Confrey, there's 'The Cat and the Mouse' by Aaron Copland, 'Cat's Waltz' by Chopin and 'Lullabies of the Cat' by Stravinsky (and that doesn't include 'What's New Pussy Cat?' recorded by Tom Jones!).

Chopin's Waltz No. 3 in F is known as the Cat's Waltz – because it was inspired by his pet cat running across the keyboard.

Cody the cat was addicted to Debussy. Whenever his master, the composer Henri Sauget, played Debussy on the piano, the little cat would roll about on the carpet with delight before leaping on to Henri's lap and licking his hands. Sadly for Henri, the cat wasn't nearly as keen on Henri's own compositions!

World leaders have historically presented statesmen and women or other world leaders with animals as gifts.

One of the first recorded was the Chinese Emperor Tien Wu Ti who sent Pekinese puppies to Japan. Henry VIII was a great horseman and often received additions to his stables from foreign dignitaries, while in 1825 an Egyptian viceroy presented King Charles X of France with a giraffe. The creature was shipped there on a converted brig – a hole was cut in the roof of the upper deck for her head to poke through.

George Washington received five hounds from the French General Lafayette, and a donkey from the King of Spain. This was the start – but not the end – of odd animals received by US presidents. President Van Buren received tiger cubs from the Sultan of Oman, while President Buchanan received elephants from the King of Siam.

Mystery writer Raymond Chandler always read the first draft of his novels to his cat, Taki

The weather reports on TV station KATU in Portland, Oregon are very popular. Not because people have an unnatural interest in the weather, but because one of the presenters is a cat.

He's Bob, a fat grey tomcat, who appears with his colleague David Apple. Whatever Bob wears reflects the forecast. If it's going to be sunny, Bob wears a little cat-size sailor suit and sunglasses; earmuffs and a scarf if snow's on the way. And if it's going to be raining cats and dogs, he sports a little raincoat and hat.

The TV station does booming business in its line of Bob the Weather Cat badges, bumper stickers and posters. As for Bob himself, well he seems unfazed by his popularity, even though he receives thousands of letters, some of which have included marriage proposals!

Strelka was the name of the Samoyed husky bitch who travelled in Sputnik V and returned safely to earth. In a gesture of friendship the Russians presented one of her puppies, Pushinka, to Caroline Kennedy in 1961 (the name Pushinka means 'fluffy' in Russian). However, before Caroline got the dog, the CIA insisted on checking it thoroughly for bugs (not fleas – the electronic kind!).

During the French Wars of Marlborough in the early eighteenth century, a chimp was brought to England by a wealthy merchant as a pet. Not having the first clue as to how smart a chimp can be, the owner took no real precautions and at the first opportunity the chimp escaped into the countryside around London. Once out in the wilds, the chimpanzee made the mistake of wandering into a rural town – and was immediately mistaken for a French spy and captured. No one in the town had ever seen a chimpanzee – or, for that matter, a Frenchman before, and so quite naturally assumed they must be one and the same! The unfortunate chimp was held under arrest, brought before the court as a French spy, convicted and imprisoned!

When guinea pigs were first brought back to Europe from South America, the fascinating little rodents became so popular that religious painters started changing the nativity scenes they were producing. Instead of a donkey, the infant Jesus was now visited by the Three Wise Men – and a guinea pig!

The French author Claude Farrère was asleep when his normally docile cat, Kare Kedi, woke up in the middle of the night and jumped on her master's bed. Her fur stood up and she stared wide-eyed at one of the walls. Then she began pacing about, all the time howling. After a few moments she leapt forward, turned a somersault and ended up in the arms of her startled owner.

Claude could see no reason for this behaviour. There were no other sounds and he tried to settle her down. He was most concerned that her howling might have woken his neighbour.

The next morning Claude found out that at the exact time of his cat's odd behaviour, his neighbour had been robbed and silently murdered in his bed.

'Even the smallest
feline is a work of art'
LEONARDO DA VINCI

One of the most talented dogs in showbusiness was a Samoyed bitch named Tundra who could respond to 200 different voice commands and 60 hand signals. She appeared in countless TV commercials and was a regular cast member of the American series, *Love Boat* where she was supplied with her own personal hairdresser and limo. In 1989 Tundra was earning $1,000 – not a week, but per day!

Although most US presidents have kept animals of one sort or another at the White House, Calvin Coolidge outdid them all. His menagerie included a bear cub, a donkey, a wallaby, two lion cubs, an antelope, a hippopotamus and a racoon called Rebecca, whom the First Lady used to take for walks around the White House on a lead.

Lions, leopards and pumas all go silly when they catch a whiff of catnip – just like domestic cats!

The *Daily Local News* of West Chester, Pennsylvania runs an obituary column with a difference – it's for pets. According to the newspaper's editor, John DeSanto, at first the column (called 'Pause to Remember') created quite a stir in the town. People questioned its value and wondered sarcastically if it would feature road kills. However, John had the last laugh. Since the pet obituaries appeared, the paper's circulation has increased by more than 10 per cent!

Sigmund Freud's daughter Anna owned an Alsatian named Wolf when they lived in Vienna. One day the dog bolted out of the house, apparently scared by gunshots fired outside.

Anna and her father searched everywhere for Wolf, but to no avail. Then, in the middle of that night, the doorbell rang. It was a taxi driver who'd stopped to let a passenger out on the other side of Vienna when Wolf jumped in and refused to get out. Apparently, Wolf just sat there with his head held high, pawing at his neck. At first the cab driver thought he was injured – perhaps that he'd cut or hurt his throat, but then the penny dropped. Wolf was indicating the tag attached to his collar.

The result was a cab ride straight across town and safe delivery to his owner's door.

Winston Churchill was a great animal lover and among the many pets that he owned was a cat named Mr Cat. Mr Cat had his own place at the dinner table at Churchill's country house, Blenheim, complete with best china place setting.

Adolf Hitler, on the other hand, hated cats and was a dog lover. In 1915, while serving in the First World War, Hitler was startled by a stray terrier that leapt into his foxhole in pursuit of a rat.

In a rare moment of kindness, Hitler decided to adopt the dog, which he named Fuchsl ('Little Fox'). In August 1917 a railway worker offered Hitler 200 marks to buy the dog but Hitler refused, saying that Fuchsl was priceless. A short time later, Fuchsl went missing. Hitler suspected the railway worker, but couldn't prove anything. He later recorded in his diary, 'I was desperate. The swine that stole my dog doesn't realise what he did to me!'

Sigmund Freud had a Chow called Jofi who played an important part in psychoanalysis. According to Freud's son Martin, Jofi attended all his father's sessions, and when she got up and yawned, that signalled the end of the session.

But don't think her yawning was arbitrary – and at the expense of the patients. According to Sigmund, she was usually accurate in announcing the end of a session to within a few minutes of the time he had allotted.

Cardinal Richelieu, King Louis XIII's chief minister, was so fond of cats that he couldn't work unless there were several kittens playing on his desk. Two of his favourites, Racan and Perruque (the latter word meaning wig), were born in the wig of the Marquis de Racan, much to the annoyance of the Marquis.

On one occasion, the Cardinal was visited by a foreign ambassador, but refused to get up and greet him – his excuse was that standing would have disturbed the cats sleeping on his lap. He made handsome provisions for all 14 of his cats in his will.

> 'God has created the cat to give man the pleasure of caressing a tiger'
>
> THÉOPHILE GAUTIER

The actors' union Equity was involved in a dispute with the producers of the West End musical *42nd Street* which at the time starred Frankie Vaughan. The problem didn't involve Frankie – but one of his co-stars, an Old English sheepdog/collie crossbreed called Shaggy Baggins.

Shaggy had made over 200 successful appearances when the director changed a routine. The new routine meant that, rather than Shaggy making an entrance on his own, he would have to be carried in. Since Shaggy was too heavy, he was sacked, leading his owner to sue the show for wrongful dismissal.

Unfortunately Equity weren't able to help: union membership is not open to animals.

In its history as the Prime Minister's London residence, 10 Downing Street has been home to a great many cats, but one of the most famous – if not the most long-lived – was a shorthaired tabby named Wilberforce. He arrived in 1973 while Edward Heath was in power, and stayed during the leadership of Harold Wilson, James Callaghan and Margaret Thatcher. When Wilberforce died peacefully in 1988, tributes from all the politicians that had known him flooded in. The only person not to mourn his passing was Mrs Thatcher's then press secretary, Bernard Ingham. The reason? Wilberforce gave him asthma.

The national bird of the United States wasn't always going to be the eagle. Benjamin Franklin, one of the Founding Fathers, suggested the turkey for the role, describing the eagle as 'a bird of bad moral character'

Some people find themselves in the unenviable position of having to give away their pet, for any number of reasons. Maybe they're moving, maybe their children are allergic to the pet or maybe they simply can't afford to keep it. Fortunately, most find homes with new owners or in animal shelters, but one anonymous owner (possibly one of the film crew) decided to find his cat a new home by letting it wander on to the set of *Dynasty* with a large sign around its neck saying, 'Please give me a home'.

Needless to say, filming stopped while people argued as to who would claim it. Actor John Forsythe (Blake Carrington) beat off Joan Collins and Linda Evans to win custody of the cat.

When President George Bush's biography was published in 1991 it was kept off the bestseller list by a book written by his dog, Millie, a springer spaniel! Well, when I say written by his dog, it was actually a collection of White House reminiscences supposedly dictated to his wife Barbara by Millie.

'Millie's Book', as it was called, stayed in the book charts for nearly five months and sold 400,000 copies, with royalties donated to charity.

When asked how President Bush felt about being upstaged by his dog, a White House spokesman told the press, 'This is somewhat embarrassing, but the President is taking it very well.'

The first animal superstar was definitely Rin Tin Tin. He was discovered, quite literally, in 1918 by Lee Duncan, an American pilot (and dog lover) who was inspecting an abandoned German aerodrome in Fleury, France. Sheltering in a foxhole was a German shepherd dog and her six puppies. Sharing the dogs among his colleagues, Lee kept two of the puppies for himself, a male and a female which he called Rin Tin Tin and Nanette, after two lovers in a French legend. After the war, Lee Duncan returned to the US with the puppies and showed Rin Tin Tin at several dog shows, teaching him hundreds of tricks and thus preparing him for a career on the vaudeville stage, on radio, and later in movies.

Ginger, a tomcat who kept down the mouse population in Salisbury Cathedral was immortalised in a stained-glass window in the cathedral when he died in 1988

Between 1923 and 1932, Rin Tin Tin starred in 22 films and was insured for $250,000; he even had five guard dogs of his own. Rin Tin Tin (or 'Rinty' as he was affectionately known) went on to make a total of 50 feature films, earning $44,000 per movie. In 1926, at the peak of his fame, he even won the vote for 'best actor' and by then was receiving a million fan letters a year. He was driven from the ranch where he lived to the studio in his own chauffeur-driven limousine and after a life of luxury, finally succumbed to old age in the arms of screen goddess Jean Harlow.

His son, Rin Tin Tin Junior, appeared in six films from 1933 to 1939. Rin Tin Tin III was a descendant of the original Rinty and as well as being an animal actor, served with the US Army during the Second World War in its K-9 Corps, receiving the Purple Heart. He appeared in just one 1947 film and another Rin Tin Tin (actually Golden Boy Jr) took the lead role in the 1954–59 TV series called *The Adventures of Rin Tin Tin* – 164 black and white episodes were made as well as a new radio series.

One of the reasons why the original Rin Tin Tin was such a good animal actor was his sense of timing. He rarely needed more than one take to perform a trick or stunt on cue – a lesson that many of today's actors and actresses could learn.

Another animal actor with many different identities was Tarzan's faithful companion, Cheetah the chimpanzee. Cheetah was by his side in most of the Tarzan films from 1932 to 1968, and also in the TV series starring Ron Ely as Tarzan, which ran from 1966 to 1969.

In the first films he appeared alongside Buster Crabbe and Johnny Weissmuller. Both actors were swimming champions of the day, so the scriptwriters wrote in lots of swimming scenes – without thinking if chimps could swim. Well, they don't as a rule, but no one had told that to a chimp called Jiggs, who relished the water. Jiggs could do lots of other tricks, like crawling on his belly and kissing, and the reason he looks convincing in the films is that all his best tricks were deliberately written into the scripts.

In all there were over a dozen Cheetahs. Jiggs played the part until the mid-1930s, followed by Skippy, Dinky then Zippy. A new chimp actor was cast for the late 1960s and this particular ape was almost born to play the part. His name? Cheetah. (By the way, the very first Cheetah is still alive and enjoying his retirement in Palm Springs. At the grand old age of sixty-five, he still enjoys a good cigar and the occasional beer by the pool!)

Alice, the wife of Theodore Roosevelt, kept a snake at the White House. She called it Emily Spinach, because she said it was as thin as her Aunt Emily and as green as spinach!

My favourite description of this next animal actor is 'Lassie in a wetsuit'. She made two films in 1963 and 1964 but what she's most famous for are 88 episodes of her own TV series which ran from 1964 until 1967. Who is she? Well, Flipper of course.

The creator of Flipper was an underwater stuntman called Ricou Browning. He originally tried to get the story of this lovable dolphin published but no one would take him seriously. Then he met up with a TV producer friend who read the manuscript and was willing to take a chance on a movie. At the time (1962) the talk in the movie business was that no one but an idiot would make a film about a boy and his dolphin. Just one year later they were proved very wrong indeed.

Although supposedly male, by tradition, Flipper has always been played by female dolphins. Mitzi starred in the two films; on TV it was Suzy and then Cathy in the lead role. Each Flipper was taught about 35 basic manoeuvres, like retrieving an object, swimming backwards and pushing an object along in the water with her nose. These tricks would normally take a dolphin years to perfect. However, all the trainers, led by Ricou, got into the pool with their aquatic stars and made friends with them. This close bonding helped to reduce the training period to just six months, as the dolphins enjoyed the companionship. (Before this, trainers used to stand at the poolside and give instructions and encouragement.) Ricou also accomplished a first for a trained dolphin – getting Mitzi to tow someone holding on to her fin (the 'volunteer' was his nine-year-old son, Ricky).

Ricou himself is no stranger to appearing in underwater films, having starred in one himself. Not many people recognised him, though. He was the monster from the classic 1954 film *The Creature from the Black Lagoon*!

The original cat seen lazing on the roof in the opening titles of ITV's *Coronation Street* wasn't meant to be there. It just wandered into shot as the rooftops were being filmed, had a quick snooze, and then walked off, never to be seen again.

However, in 1989 Granada TV decided that the title sequence needed renewing and they shortlisted ten hopeful cats from over 5,000 applications that poured into the studio.

Five cats were selected by TV viewers on a breakfast TV phone-in, and these finalists were screen-tested on the *Coronation Street* set, appearing in scenes with Percy Sugden and Emily Bishop and being judged on their poise as they entered the Rovers Return, walked down a street and posed on a wall. A panel of judges (including Ken Dodd and Jean Alexander, who played Hilda Ogden) then made the final decision. The winner? A three-year-old tabby tom called Frisky who lived with his owner Mrs Joyce Rimmington just outside Leeds – in a converted castle.

During the English Civil War, Roundheads thought that a poodle was in league with the devil!

The poodle was named Boye and belonged to Prince Rupert. Both he and King Charles were devoted to Boye and they even took him to church services. Prince Rupert once held a royal dinner in gratitude for Boye, who, it was thought, had brought them luck in a recent skirmish. The Roundheads who had seen Boye on the battlefield were convinced that he was Rupert's 'familiar spirit' and had been a 'handsome white lady' before being turned into a poodle.

When Boye passed away, the prince's fortunes began to change for the worse. Perhaps Boye *had* been more than he seemed . . .

Chapter Nine

TO THE RESCUE!

In 1942, Sergeant Cyril Jones was parachuted into Sumatra on a top secret mission against the invading Japanese Army. Unfortunately, things went wrong right from the start. Cyril's parachute and harness got hopelessly tangled up high in the trees and he was left dangling there for days, unable to free himself. Things looked hopeless, until he was adopted by a monkey who seemed to sense his predicament. 'We became very close friends and the monkey started bringing me bananas to eat,' Cyril recalls. 'Sometimes he would bring me bamboo shoots which he showed me how to eat.'

Eventually Cyril did manage to free himself and set off on his mission with the monkey in tow – only to be captured by a Japanese patrol and thrown into a POW camp. Sadly, it was there that he had to say goodbye to his faithful friend, chasing the monkey off into the jungle every time it appeared. 'I had to get rid of him because he turned on the Japanese soldiers every time they tried to bully me,' he says. His brave and faithful friend had to be chased away for its own protection . . .

When Perth cattle farmer Nigel Etherington found a young orphaned rock wallaby sitting on the roadside next to the body of its mother, he took pity on it and brought it back to his farm where he gave it some milk and made up a cosy bed in his bathroom. Little did he realise that in return, the very same night, the young wallaby would save his life!

As Nigel slept, some electrical wiring in his spare room caught fire, and choking black smoke spread throughout the house. Nigel might never have woken up, except for the frantic banging on his bedroom door. He staggered out of bed and found the young wallaby outside his door. The animal had been propping itself up on its tail and repeatedly kicking at the door with its hind legs. Man and wallaby then both fled outside to safety.

'As soon as I opened the door I caught sight of the little roo at my feet before I was engulfed in smoke,' says Nigel. 'The roo hopped out of the house and I followed right on his tail. If the little fellow hadn't woken me I would have died in my sleep within a few minutes. My rescue was just like you see on the TV series *Skippy the Kangaroo!*'

After that, Nigel offered the wallaby a permanent home on his farm, but the youngster voted with his outsized feet – and was last seen hopping off back into the bush.

Spike the baby greenfinch must be the luckiest bird in the world. At one day old, blind and pink and with just two little feathers jutting out from the top of his head, Spike accidentally fell out of his nest – straight into a cattery. There he lay on the ground, surrounded by no fewer than 56 gleeful cats. It should have been all over for Spike, but George the Yorkshire terrier came bounding to the rescue. She stood over the tiny fledgling, barking and growling to keep the cats at bay until Julie Carter arrived.

Julie, the owner of the Five Star Boarding Cattery in Wrawby, Lincolnshire says, 'George kept barking at me and I went to see what she'd found. The poor little bird was as good as dead, but George was brilliant. She stood there and just wouldn't let the cats get anywhere near it.'

Julie nursed Spike back to health on a diet of worms, crushed biscuits and water, and now the little fledgling and George are the best of friends. 'George is just like a surrogate mother to Spike,' says Julie. 'She barks whenever Spike needs feeding, and growls if any cats come near!'

It was the most terrifying moment in Mark Richardson's life. The young diver from Colchester was swimming in the Red Sea off the coast of the Sinai Peninsula when, without warning, he was attacked by a shark. 'I didn't see anything strange, but suddenly I felt something bite my left side and it punctured my lung,' he recalls. 'I saw it then for the first time and managed to punch it on the nose, but it took another bite from my chest. I was struggling and screaming, waiting for it to come back and finish me off. I thought I was a goner.'

The next moment three bottlenose dolphins raced to Mark's aid. As he waited for the shark to attack, the dolphins swam around him in a tight circle, flapping their fins and tails frantically to keep the shark at bay – exactly as if they were protecting one of their own babies. They kept it up until Mark's friends arrived in their boat to drag him from the water and race him to hospital.

Martin Berry's guide dog Innis not only changed his life – he also saved it. When Martin collapsed unconscious at his home in Luton after failing to turn his gas cooker off properly, Innis brought him round with a succession of big sloppy slurping kisses. The two then escaped. 'I would have died if it wasn't for Innis,' Martin admits. 'He's a hero!'

Every year, tragedies occur when dogs fall through the ice on a frozen pond or a lake and their owners try to rescue them. In 1996, however, two dogs rushed out on to the ice to save their master instead. Jim Gilchrist of Innisfil, Ontario had unwisely gone out on to the ice covering Lake Simcoe. The ice had cracked, tipping him into the water. Tara, his four-year-old Rottweiler bounded out to the rescue, only to plunge in herself. As man and dog struggled together in the icy waters, Jim's other dog, a one-year-old golden retriever called Tiree, seemed to comprehend the danger. She approached the hole in the ice timidly, crouching down and spreading her weight to avoid breaking the ice. Keeping a firm grip on Tiree's collar to prevent himself going under, Jim managed to push Tara back up on to the ice. He then clutched hold of both dogs' collars and between them the two dogs managed to haul him from the water. For their courage and intelligence, Tara and Tiree were honoured at Canada's 28th annual Purina Animal Hall of Fame Awards.

Here's one daring rescue you won't see re-enacted on BBC's 999 programme! In 1987, the Padham fire brigade were called to Pennyfold Farm in Hapton, Lancashire – to rescue a cow which had strayed into a slurry pit. Rescue lines were strung over the pit and then the firemen waded out waist deep into the liquid manure to reach the cow, who was stuck fast. A valiant tug of war ensued, with firemen regularly losing their grip and slipping backwards under the slurry as they fought for two hours to free the cow. Eventually they succeeded, clambered out of the slurry pit after the cow had been saved, and then turned the fire hoses on themselves for a good 10 minutes to try and wash away the almighty stench. That didn't work: the unmistakable odour lingered on the unfortunate firemen for days afterwards!

Snort the potbellied pig lived with her owners, Deborah and Collin Stolpe, in a mobile home. One night in November 1995, they had checked into a trailer park in Colorado and settled down to sleep. In the middle of the night, Deborah was awoken by Snort bellowing at the top of her lungs and running up and down the aisle. Deborah tried to take Snort outside, but the pig refused to leave. Worried now that something was seriously wrong, Deborah returned to find her husband having violent convulsions. Now Deborah began to feel sick and light-headed too. Luckily, she realised what Snort had been trying to warn her about. The mobile home's heater outlet had become clogged, and lethal carbon monoxide fumes were filling their home. Snort's warning had come just in time and, with the help of other campers, Deborah was able to rescue her husband. Despite having had the opportunity to leave the vehicle and stay in the fresh air, Snort had stubbornly chosen to stay inside and keep on warning her owners. She was later rewarded with a lifesaving award from the American Humane Association.

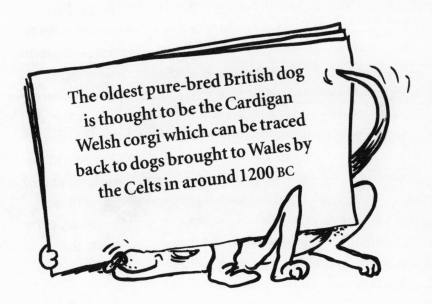

The oldest pure-bred British dog is thought to be the Cardigan Welsh corgi which can be traced back to dogs brought to Wales by the Celts in around 1200 BC

For a long time after King William III's death, Jacobite rebels drank a toast to 'the little gentleman in black velvet'. This was their name for the mole whose molehill tripped up the king's horse, sending William crashing to the ground and breaking his collarbone, an injury which ultimately resulted in his death.

It was in the early days of the First World War and the elite Vienna Cavalry were finishing their preparations before being sent to the front.

One cold night there was a scratching at the mess door, and a steward opened it to see a thin, starving puppy looking up at him. Before he knew it, the puppy had run inside, to enjoy the warmth of the officers' mess.

Although food was in short supply – even for officers – Captain Karl Weiss adopted the stray dog and gave him scraps from his own meals. He called him Hans, and the two became inseparable.

When the regiment left for the front, Hans went with them and lived in Captain Weiss' tent. One day in 1915, after a particularly fierce battle, Captain Weiss did not return and was feared dead – though his body was not found among the dead or wounded.

His comrades had an idea. They would use Hans to try and locate his beloved master. Hans set off round the battlefield with the other officers in pursuit. He sniffed around the heaps of corpses strewn everywhere. One heap in particular made him stop. He stood up on his back legs, trying to knock the topmost bodies down to the ground.

The officers joined in and, to their amazement, found Captain Weiss pinned under the bodies. He was alive, but breathing very weakly. His comrades rushed him to a field hospital and surgeons later told him he would certainly have died from his wounds if he'd remained undiscovered. Hans had repaid the kindness shown to him by the captain by saving his life. The two of them survived the war and remained firm friends for many years afterwards.

Chip was a collie belonging to Nick Conner and the two of them would often go for strolls along the beach near where they lived in West Sussex. Their favourite game was having Nick throw a ball out to sea and Chip splashing through the surf, then swimming out to the ball and bringing it back in his teeth.

On one occasion, Nick threw the ball but Chip didn't bring it back. He swam past it towards what looked like some rags bobbing up and down in the water. Whatever it was, Nick saw Chip gently clasp it in his mouth and then swim back with it, before depositing it on the beach.

It was a seagull – one that had been caught in some fishing line and was unable to move its wings. Nick was able to untangle it, watched closely by Chip. At last the bird was freed and after resting on the sand for a while it took to the air.

As if thanking Chip, it circled the little dog twice before heading back out to sea. Satisfied with his good deed, Chip then got on with his game.

Like most diabetics, Athena Lethcoe of Nikisiki in Alaska has to be constantly aware of her blood sugar level. If it gets too low, she can slip into a diabetic coma, and that's exactly what happened one fateful day in March 1993.

That afternoon Athena had felt tired and decided to lie down for a quick nap in the basement bedroom. She was rudely woken up by Silver, her pet collie, shaking her violently. Normally, when Athena went for a rest, Silver would never disturb her. This time something was obviously wrong – but what?

Athena tried to figure it out but felt herself drifting back to sleep – only to be awakened once more by Silver, who was now barking loudly. Again, Athena tried to work out what the matter was but she couldn't think straight. Then suddenly she realised what had happened. Her blood sugar level was running dangerously low. She had to do something or she would die.

The problem was that she was too weak to get up. She knew she had sugar in the kitchen but the problem was getting up the basement stairs.

Silver kept nudging Athena, even pawing her to encourage her to get up. She managed to slide off the bed and crawl along the basement floor, helped along by Silver who nudged her with his snout each time she stopped. The biggest hurdle was the staircase. Each time Athena tried to pull herself up, one step at a time, she would lose her grip and fall backwards. But Silver was there, steadying her and stopping her from falling all the way down again.

After what seemed like hours Athena reached the top and crawled to the kitchen on her stomach, her strength fading fast. But, encouraged by Silver urging her on, she managed to open the fridge door and slurp down a carton of sweet, flavoured milk.

This revitalised her sufficiently to call for an ambulance, which arrived shortly afterwards. While she was waiting, Silver stayed by her side, just to make sure she didn't pass out.

Athena owed her life to Silver, the collie who sensed that something was wrong and knew what he must do to save his mistress.

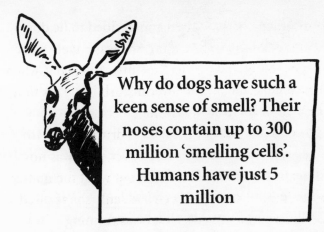

Why do dogs have such a keen sense of smell? Their noses contain up to 300 million 'smelling cells'. Humans have just 5 million

Albert Smith was at his home next to the lower Elwah River in Washington when he saw a tugboat floundering in the stormy sea off nearby Angeles Point. Gale force winds and 20-foot waves were tossing the *Barney Junior* around and she was rapidly taking on water.

Wasting no time, Albert rushed out of his house and saddled his small, stocky pony, Shotgun. Drenched to the skin, she carried Albert through the storm to the shore, where he could just make out two figures standing on the deck of the tug, a quarter of a mile out to sea.

Albert and Shotgun galloped into the roaring surf. A sandy ledge ran along the shore so the pony could wade quite a way out. On seeing Shotgun, the two sailors launched a small rubber dinghy. Albert's plan was to ride Shotgun as near as he could and then tow the dinghy to the shore. No one would be able to swim to safety in these conditions.

Battling against the wind and the waves, Albert managed to get hold of the line the sailors had thrown and tie it to Shotgun's saddle. Despite the waves crashing around them and the strain of the dinghy's weight, Shotgun managed to keep her balance and began heaving herself towards the shore. Although struggling with the weight she was towing, Shotgun was making headway – then disaster struck! A huge wave from nowhere crashed down on horse and rider, sweeping Albert from the saddle. Shotgun continued on riderless, still heaving on the line attached to the dinghy, and slowly but surely she pulled the two sailors to the safety of the beach. While all three were trying to recover, a lone drenched figure pulled himself wearily out of the water and collapsed next to them – it was Albert Smith, who had also survived the terrible storm!

Albert made the headlines for his courageous action but tried to play down all the publicity. After all, he said, Shotgun was the true hero of the hour.

Trainwreck is an unusual name for a dog – but not when you consider the circumstances of his life.

A driver on one of the trains that travels from South Bend and Michigan City in Indiana reported that he'd accidentally hit and killed a dog that had been walking across the tracks.

But when engineer Ted Nekvasil travelled past the same spot a week later he was amazed to see the dog still alive – he had raised himself up on his front legs as the train passed, but his back half didn't appear to be moving.

Ted stopped the train and ran back to the spot, where he found a weak, injured German shepherd. He radioed the depot with the news, as he had to continue on with his train. Soon two railway workers came out, befriended the dog and took him to an animal clinic in Michigan City where he was examined by Dr Christine Ellis.

Amazingly, Christine found the dog had no broken bones, but his muscles had atrophied from lying in the cold, without food for a week. She considered putting him to sleep, but there seemed to be a spark of life in his big eyes and a determined 'never say die' expression on his emaciated face.

Although she thought it would be futile, Dr Ellis embarked on a programme of treatment and exercise to build up the dog's strength, especially his muscles. To her delight, his appetite soon improved and he made slow but steady progress on the way back to health.

Each day Dr Ellis would go to the clinic and ask how the train wreck dog was progressing – and that's how he got his name.

After months, Trainwreck was able to walk again. His owner couldn't be traced so he was given a new home on a nearby farm. Here he leads an active life after his miraculous recovery – and he stays well away from railway lines, as you can imagine.

It's amazing how family pets somehow form a deep, unspoken bond with children in the home. They seem to develop a sixth sense for vulnerable youngsters and make it their job to look out for them. Sometimes, they can literally be life savers. Little two-year-old Tiffany Bartens was asleep in her cot at her family home in Pembroke Docks in Dyfed when she suddenly stopped breathing. Her parents, Carsten and Jocavia, were fast asleep and had no idea how much danger their daughter was in – but Beethoven, their Siamese cat did. Although he had been fast asleep downstairs, somehow, Beethoven knew that Tiffany was in trouble. He raced upstairs and started frantically scratching at the nursery door and screeching with all his might. The commotion woke Tiffany's parents and her mother was just in time to bring her round with the kiss of life and heart massage. No one can explain how Beethoven knew Tiffany was in danger, they're just glad she did. 'We owe Tiffany's life to Beethoven. Those extra few seconds he gave us made all difference,' says Jocavia. 'It was just like a scene from Lassie – and Beethoven turned into a real-life hero!'

A young boy was plucked to safety by his family's Rottweiler, Troy, in an extraordinary story that took place in January 1981. The boy, his stepfather and their dog were out walking around the Kings Mill reservoir near their home in Mansfield, Nottinghamshire. The boy had run off ahead to explore the various jetties that jutted out into the water when he lost his footing and fell into the freezing water. He was wearing a thick coat and boots which soon became waterlogged, pulling him under. What's more, he couldn't swim.

His stepfather knew he couldn't reach his son in time, but quick thinking saved the day. He let Troy off his leash, pointed ahead to the struggling boy and shouted, 'Fetch!'

Without hesitating, Troy bounded into the water, swam towards the boy and grabbed his coat collar in his powerful jaws just as he was about to go under and pulled him safely to the shore.

Cats' ears have over thirty different muscles so that they can instantly turn to hear sounds coming from any direction!

Slowly Cat is an odd name for a pet but it summed up the casual attitude of the moggie belonging to Virgil and Linda McMillian of Arkansas. Every night Slowly Cat was let out but would amble back home again after five minutes. One very cold night, he didn't return. Virgil and Linda searched the neighbourhood but couldn't find any trace of him. They were especially worried since the temperature had fallen to 12 degrees below freezing. They hoped that Slowly Cat had found shelter, wherever he was, and decided to call off the search that night.

They began their hunt again the next morning. Virgil was examining some ground to the rear of their house when he came across an old sack. He didn't think anything of it until out popped Slowly Cat. He looked at his master, stretched and then disappeared back into the sack.

Virgil was really pleased his pet was safe, but when he opened the sack to bring him out again, he discovered an abandoned baby boy lying at the bottom. Slowly Cat was curled up around him and licking the poor child's face. Virgil rushed home with the baby, who was taken by ambulance to a nearby hospital.

Although his tiny heart had almost stopped beating with the cold, doctors managed to stabilise him and he slowly made a full recovery. It was clear that if Slowly Cat had not snuggled into the sack with the baby, the child would have died. It was only the cat's body heat and the licking that had kept the boy alive.

In March 1834, two young boys fell into the Grosvenor Canal near Pimlico. Neither could swim and both immediately disappeared under the brackish, filthy water. Luckily an actor was walking his Newfoundland dog along the towpath and spotted the children going under. The dog – appropriately enough named Hero – jumped in and started swimming about but couldn't find the boys. His owner began flinging pebbles into the water where the boys had last been seen and the dog dived for them, emerging with first one boy and then the other, in rapid succession. Both boys' lives were saved and Hero was guest of honour at a special society dinner held just for him.

Feeding the seagulls regularly certainly paid off for pensioners Rachel and June Flynn. There was one extra-friendly gull they got to know well and called Nancy. One day in 1980, Rachel was walking along the cliffs near her home in Cape Cod when she lost her footing. She pitched down a 30-foot embankment, ending up sprawled on a deserted stretch of beach, unable to move. As she looked up, a seagull swooped down and started to hover above her. It looks like Nancy, she thought, and in her semi-delirious state she cried out, 'For God's sake, Nancy, get help!'

A mile away, Rachel's sister June was cooking in her kitchen when a gull started rapping on her window with its beak, flapping its wings frantically and cawing at the top of its voice. June tried to shoo the bird off, but it persisted. After about a quarter of an hour, June finally decided that the bird was trying to tell her something.

Putting on her coat and boots, June followed the bird across the cliffs. From time to time it would stop and wheel in the air, as if making sure it was being followed. Then it started hovering and, looking down, June saw her sister Rachel lying on the beach below. She quickly called the fire brigade and Rachel was taken to hospital with a badly twisted knee and some bruising.

In all of Shakespeare's plays there is only one dog, Crab, who appears in *The Two Gentlemen of Verona*

On 17 October 1989, northern California was hit by a tremendous earthquake that terrified humans and pets alike.

Reona, a two-and-a-half year old Rottweiler owned by Jim Patton of Watsonville, appeared to be traumatised after the first shock hit. She bounded out of the door and leapt over five consecutive garden fences – something she'd never done before in her life.

Jim thought Reona had been spooked but she'd actually heard cries for help. These cries had come from five-year-old Vivian Cooper, a neighbour's child who was standing terrified in the middle of her parents' kitchen while objects crashed down all around her. Reona raced in and pushed her to safety against some cabinets, actually sitting on her to protect her. Seconds later, another even more violent shock wave sent a heavy microwave oven crashing down from the top of a refrigerator, to land exactly where Vivian had been standing just moments before.

A wild dolphin saved the lives of three small children off the Java coast in 1988. The children had been flung into the sea by their father as the ferry they were on caught fire. The dolphin used his nose to nudge and cajole the children to a waiting life-raft.

Just before a devastating earthquake struck Peking in July 1976, a golden retriever called Lisa gave staff at the British Embassy a valuable early warning. Despite all efforts, she would not stop leaping about and barking. This convinced officials that something terrible was about to happen and they quickly evacuated the building. Moments later, the quake hit with 11,000 times the destructive power of the Hiroshima bomb. Because they were outside and away from the buildings, the people Lisa had warned were saved.

Strulli the Alsatian could sense something was wrong. He and his master, Josef Becker had stopped off for a drink in a local inn, but Strulli didn't like it at all. He howled. He ran round in circles. He tugged at his master's clothes and jumped up at the walls until Josef lost his patience and threw the dog outside.

Undeterred, Strulli came racing back in through another entrance and resumed grabbing hold of Josef's jacket in his jaws and trying to pull him off his stool. He gave up and went outside with him. Two minutes later, the inn collapsed, killing nine people inside.

Rex the black and white collie saved the life of three-year-old Roland not once, not twice, not three times but an amazing four times! The dog was owned by a family in Ferriby, East Yorkshire and became especially attached to his owner's grandson, Roland.

Roland was a bit of a terror, wandering off and getting into trouble at the drop of a hat, so Rex really had his work cut out for him! The first time Roland toddled off, he ended up strolling along the middle of a busy main street with cars and lorries swerving all around him. Rex sprang into the road to join him and then, watching out for gaps in the traffic, gently eased and nudged the boy back to the safety of the pavement.

From them on, Roland's parents watched him like a hawk, but the junior Houdini still managed to give them the slip. Just a few weeks later, he escaped and tottered into a brickworks. Seeing the brick pond, he immediately jumped in and sank. Rex plunged in and, gripping the boy by his collar, dragged him out again.

Despite his parents' best efforts, Roland escaped for a third time and went missing. Villagers quickly formed a search party but there was no sign of him. Night was beginning to fall, and so was the temperature.

There seemed no hope for Roland, but as the sun came up a farmer's wife saw a little boy being pushed towards the safety of the farm by a black and white collie! To judge by the footprints the terrible Roland had gone down to the treacherous banks of the Humber. Rex had followed him down there and enticed him away to the comparative safety of the meadows. The two had spent the night there, huddled up together, with Rex keeping his young charge warm. However, at dawn, Roland had woken up and gone scampering off again. This time he strolled on to a main railway line. Rex had once again guided him away, and had led him to the safety of the farmhouse.

Chapter Ten

PIGS MIGHT FLY

It was the most unusual request the Barratt's showroom salesman had ever heard. Lisa and Ricci Sayer said they'd be interested in buying one of the £84,000 four-bedroomed properties on the new site at Measham in Leicestershire – but only if it could be supplied ready fitted with pig flaps. The salesman checked. No, they were quite sure they didn't want cat flaps. They wanted pig flaps, for Twiggy, their pet Vietnamese potbellied pig so that she could stroll into the conservatory or garden whenever she pleased.

'Twiggy is quite a large animal and it helps if she can come and go as she pleases,' says Mrs Sayer. 'This way she can roam in and out at will. She certainly doesn't bring dirt into the house. In fact, it's quite funny to see her tiptoeing around any muddy patches in the garden.'

After being assured that the Sayers weren't telling him 'porkies', site manager Phil Clarke delivered their home to them complete with two exceptionally large lockable pig flaps as requested. 'We don't mind making the odd adjustment here and there to make sure the whole family is happy,' he says; 'even the pets.'

The best man was a parrot, the maid of honour was an iguana and the happy couple were two cats – there was certainly nothing typical about the wedding which took place on 5 October 1996 at the Phoebus Amphitheatre in Bangkok,

Thailand! The bride and groom – Ploy and Phet – were both 'diamond-eye' cats, which means they suffer from a form of glaucoma. Diamond-eyes are believed to be especially lucky in Thailand, and the owner of Phet (the bridegroom) believed that good luck helped his import-export company to thrive and prosper. To celebrate, he threw his beloved cat the most spectacular wedding he could lay on. Ploy, the bride, was flown to the wedding by helicopter while Phet arrived on the back seat of a Rolls-Royce flanked by a motorcycle escort. Both cats were given gold rings for their paws and then, while 500 human guests, including the Thai deputy Prime Minister, enjoyed a lavish wedding banquet, the two cats were sent off on a luxury honeymoon cruise along the Choi Phya river.

And the best wedding present of all? After it was all over, both cats were to have corrective eye surgery on their 'diamond eyes' so that they would be able to see normally again.

Fancy owning a pig? Pigs are becoming increasingly popular pets because of their friendliness and keen intelligence. However, would you believe that before you take Babe or Porky for walkies, you'll need to obtain a special pig-walking licence from the Ministry of Agriculture!

The people of Lancashire and Yorkshire have always enjoyed a friendly rivalry – but now even the bats in the two counties are at it! They tell me that bat colonies in Yorkshire and Lancashire each have distinct regional accents in the sounds they make, so bats in Yorkshire can't understand what their fellow bats over in Lancashire are on about. This means that the two species don't like each other and won't interbreed.

Sir Isaac Newton invented the cat flap!

It was a situation every woman dreads. Estelle Littmann was driving alone in her car on a deserted back road in Montgomery, Alabama, when a brown van pulled up alongside her. The driver leaned out of the window and shouted at her. Thankfully, she had the window rolled up so she couldn't hear any of the abuse and profanities he was hurling at her. Estelle tried ignoring him, focusing on the road straight ahead. Then the van swerved in front of her, flashed its brake lights, blocked her way and signalled for her to stop. Instead, she slammed her foot on the accelerator, swerved around the van and raced away. The van set off after her. She could see its headlights flashing in her rear-view mirror as she tried to get away, driving faster and faster. She was now in the outskirts of town, and made for a housing development where she knew a security guard would be on duty. As she pulled up next to the guard, the van swept by with a few last blasts on its horn.

As the dazed woman staggered from her car, the security guard looked at her and said, 'Ma'am, are you aware that you've got a cat on the top of your car?'

'I turned around and there, spreadeagled on the roof and clutching hold of my roof rack for dear life was my black and white tomcat Ronald,' Estelle recalled later. 'The poor baby had just had the ride from Hell and he looked like he was frozen solid!'

(If you feel guilty smiling at that story, don't worry. It took Ronald a few days to thaw out, but apart from that he suffered no lasting ill-effects and apparently doesn't hold it against Estelle!)

A very special kitten was born in North Jutland, Denmark, in November 1995. Pia Biscoff found him abandoned in an old hayloft and immediately took a shine to him. Like all kittens he was irresistibly cute and insatiably curious. He also just happened to be bright green. No one can explain why the kitten had luxuriant bright green fur – and it didn't seem to bother him – but he's got veterinary experts the world over in a spin. Who knows, this could be the start of something. Anyone like a short-haired Chartreuse?

You might have considered learning another language, like French or German, but have you ever considered learning to speak Cat? Linguist Alexandra Sellers says that, after eight years of intense research, she's rediscovered the 'lost language of the cat' and, what's more, you can learn it too. In her book, *Spoken Cat*, she provides all the key purrs, miaows and chirps necessary for you to have simple, everyday conversations with your cat – and even gives home lessons for more ambitious would-be cat translators. Alexandra says she learned the language by interviewing dozens of cats. Cats, she claims, have much to teach us – especially about caring for our environment. 'They're particularly horrified that our sewage goes back into our drinking water,' she says. 'That, for a cat, is completely beyond endurance!'

The fact that they live in a high rise apartment didn't stop a Hindu couple in Singapore from following tradition. To have their home blessed, they hired a cow and a calf for $480, and had them brought all the way up in the lift to their new home, where the blessing was carried out. The couple also incurred an extra $200 cost – for professional carpet cleaners to clear up afterwards!

The Roman emperor Nero had ceremonial mules fitted out in miniature boots with solid silver soles. Not to be outdone, his wife Poppaea then went and had boots made for *her* mules – with solid gold soles!

Dim-witted thieves who raided Bob Hodgson's pigeon loft in Ryton, Tyne and Wear in 1997, clearly hadn't thought things through. They snatched 40 birds, but within just a few days almost all the flock had returned home safely again.

'I don't know what they expected,' said Bob later. 'You don't have to be a criminal mastermind to realise homing pigeons fly home!'

A police spokesman commented: 'Perhaps this gives you some idea of the level of intelligence of some of the thieves we have to deal with here.'

Lambs have a sweet tooth! That's according to research carried out by the Macaulay Land Use Research Institute in Aberdeen. They particularly like strawberries, oranges, caramel, vanilla-flavoured feed, and are also partial to the odd toffee. When they grow up, just like us, their palates become more discriminating. The older sheep prefer truffles and a hint of garlic with their meals. Earlier research has already shown that cows and pigs enjoy the same sort of sweet and tasty treats we humans like – but scientists didn't expect sheep to be such demanding gourmets as well!

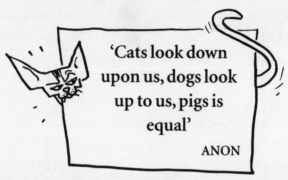

'Cats look down upon us, dogs look up to us, pigs is equal'

ANON

Before clocks, the ancient Chinese discovered that cats could make good timekeepers – or more specifically, their eyes could. At sunrise, a cat's pupils were quite dilated – these gradually became narrower towards midday, then widened again up until sunset.

With the skilful interpretation of a cat's eyes, it was possible to be accurate to the nearest hour.

In ancient Babylon, it was considered an omen if a dog relieved himself on you. If the dog was black or white, then you'd have bad luck. However, having a red dog wee on you meant happiness and prosperity (not forgetting a visit to the laundry).

If you've ever wondered where the expression 'to let the cat out of the bag' comes from, you may be interested to learn that it refers to a medieval con trick. On market days, piglets were often sold in bags. Tricksters would sometimes put a cat into the bag instead and sell it to anyone too dim-witted to check. Incidentally, the old English word for a bag was a 'poke' – which is why you should never buy a 'pig in a poke'.

In France during the Middle Ages, a cat seen sitting by the door of a church before a wedding was a sign of bad luck. In addition, if an engaged girl accidentally trod on a cat's tail, she was advised to put off her wedding for a whole year.

In ancient Siam, it was customary for a live cat to be buried with the body of a dead member of royalty. But don't worry – the tomb had small holes drilled in it so that the cat could wriggle its way free. When it did eventually emerge, temple priests believed that the soul of the dead person had passed into the cat's body and it was treated with due reverence and respect.

Yorkshire still employs an official wolf-catcher, despite the fact that the last wolf in Britain was reported in 1864!

Music hall star George Robey spent months working on a trained cat act – which was asking for trouble right from the start. He eventually succeeded in training them for a complicated and dazzling routine and the opening night arrived. The curtain went up and there was George and there were his 12 trained cats, sitting in their opening positions on 12 little chairs but before George could utter a word, someone in the audience made a loud hissing sound. The cats panicked. They all flew in different directions – some into the orchestra pit, others backstage and still others up the stage curtains, yowling and screeching. Months of work ruined in an instant. George was about to slink off stage when the audience began to roar with laughter and applaud wildly. They thought it was the best opening joke they'd ever seen!

A Belgian sheepdog called Corsair escaped from a cage at Chicago's busy O'Hare Airport and was seen by ground staff scampering across the main runway towards a hangar. His capture was given priority and all other work stopped as frantic United Airlines staff shouted his name along with 'Here boy!', 'Come on!', and other words of canine encouragement. None of these had any effect – until someone realised that being a Belgian dog, he only understood commands in French . . .

The language barrier was also firmly in place when a Surrey farmer travelled to Wales to see a sheepdog in action. He was impressed, handed over £65 there and then and brought him back home. The problem was that the dog had been trained to understand Welsh commands and when the new owner shouted orders at him in English, the dog just sat there, looking confused – some said, even sheepish!

You'd think that professional dog handlers would have more sense, but no. In 1983 Wayne County police in New Jersey paid nearly $3,000 for a highly trained German shepherd and had her shipped over from Germany. It was only after a few days of 'acting dumb' that someone realised that she'd been trained to follow orders in German . . .

In Nairobi police arrested sister Irene, a nun, for smuggling 6,000 bees into Kenya under her habit. Apparently she wanted the beeswax to make candles . . .

Here's a cow who didn't jump over the moon – she just flew in an aeroplane. Her name was Ollie and she was the first cow to fly – in February 1931 – as part of a promotional campaign for Elm Farm of St Louis, Missouri. Ollie, watched by reporters, was milked in-flight and her milk put into containers that were dropped by parachute on to surprised residents on the ground.

Don't thank the Romans or ancient Greeks for introducing the concept of mud baths: thank pigs. Baldred was the son of a king of the Britons who was sent to study in Greece. There he caught leprosy, for which there was no known cure. However, noticing that the mud seemed to be good for the pig's skin, Baldred tried the same. The mud bath worked – Baldred's leprosy was greatly relieved and the site of the mud bath became the site for the City of Bath, founded in 863 BC.

When Captain Cook landed in Australia and got his first good look at a kangaroo, he couldn't believe his eyes. 'What do you call that thing?' he asked his aborigine guide. 'Kangaroo', the guide replied – and the name stuck. Only some years later did Captain Cook find out that 'kangaroo' actually meant 'I can't understand a word you're saying' . . .

Some fishermen in Nova Scotia are so superstitious that they immediately turn around and sail their boat back to dock if anyone on board mentions the word 'pig'

A lawyer who loves dogs manages to combine the best of both worlds. She's Linda Cawley, an American attorney who specialises in dog law. Most of her work involves disputes over ownership, trust funds left in wills for pets, veterinary insurance – even dogs mislaid (or actually lost) by airlines. One of her strangest cases, however, involved her representing a defendant accused of barking too loudly. Except the defendant wasn't a dog – it was a man!

The man lived next door to a noisy dog and one day, when it barked at him, he barked back. This made the dog bark louder but the man gave as good as he got. Eventually, the man and the dog were barking at each other at the top of their voices. The police were called and he was charged with harassing the animal.

The case went to court but Linda got him off. The judge agreed with her defence: that the man was only exercising his freedom of speech!

The mighty Habsburg Empire which ruled much of Europe for centuries was plagued by ravens – or rather, the bad omens which arrived with ravens. These huge birds were seen after every battle the Habsburgs lost; they flew over Marie Antoinette while she was taken to the guillotine and they appeared above the streets in Sarajevo just before the assassination of Archduke Ferdinand, which started the First World War.

Pet therapy dogs are now helping to cheer up residents in Connecticut nursing homes by putting on a very special show – of square dancing! The dogs and their owners have got together to form 'The Woofing Hoofers', the world's first canine dance troupe, and they're proving a big hit with the sick and the elderly they entertain. No matter how down they may be feeling, no one can help being reduced to tears of laughter by the sight of 16 pet therapy dogs square dancing. It's a powerful tonic. And the 'Woofing Hoofers' have big plans to expand their show. Next on the list? A 'big band' routine and a display of traditional Greek dancing!

In 1994, Ugandan police hunted in vain for a lunatic who was shooting gorillas with tranquilliser darts and then dressing them up as clowns while they were asleep. The beasts would later regain consciousness wearing big red noses, pointed hats and satin tunics with fluffy pom-pom 'buttons'. They were not amused . . .

Camels were first introduced to the United States in 1856 at the request of Jefferson Davis, then the Secretary of War. He saw potential in using them for carrying supplies between cavalry forts in the desert regions of the American South-West.

In theory this was a good plan. The camel is superior to the horse and mule in that it can go without food or water for up to two weeks, can live off sparse vegetation and is capable of carrying heavier loads. I said 'in theory' because as soon as the camels arrived in Texas from North Africa, the US Army's problems began.

First of all, no US Army handler could deal with the camels. Camels are known the world over for their bad temper and their spitting. They also smelled like nothing on earth and no one wanted anything to do with them. Even cattle panicked at the sight of the strange creatures.

Secondly, the Arab handlers who came over with the camels couldn't speak English and the Americans couldn't speak Arabic. All instructions took the form of sign and hand gestures and this led to all sorts of confusions.

But the biggest problem arose when the Arabs received their daily ration of beer. The Americans didn't know they were teetotal and to avoid appearing rude, the handlers used to discreetly tip the alcohol away – into the camels' drinking pails! Ordinarily this wouldn't have been a problem but the US soldiers saw this and thought that beer must be an important part of the camels' diet. After that they filled the camels' pails up with beer on a daily basis. What's more, the camels loved it.

You can guess the rest. The camels were hardly able to stand up, let alone walk straight. They were sluggish and even more bad-tempered – sozzled ships of the desert!

During the Civil War the camels were captured by the Confederate Army – then recaptured by Union soldiers. Many escaped into the desert where they reverted to their wild (and sober) state. Small bands of them could often be seen roaming in isolated areas. The last of the original 79 was still wandering free as late as 1903, clearly recognisable by the army brand on its flank. Whether it had recovered from its hangover by then is not reported!

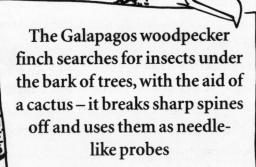

The Galapagos woodpecker finch searches for insects under the bark of trees, with the aid of a cactus – it breaks sharp spines off and uses them as needle-like probes

In February 1983, a Masai tribesman was arrested for trying to strangle a stuffed lion exhibit in the foyer of the Nairobi Ministry of Tourism office. His excuse was that his brother had been killed by a lion and this was his way of avenging his brother's death. When asked if he knew that the lion was stuffed he said no. Apparently he thought it was 'just a bit docile'.

Ralf McGreggor is a Pennsylvanian dairy farmer whose herd always produces a high yield of good quality milk. His secret? A diet of chocolate for the cows, introduced in the form of ground-up *KitKats* and other snacks. Ralf claims the chocolate provides twice the energy of corn – and the cows love it.

A farmer in Wisconsin swears by *his* method of increasing milk production – cow bras. These specially designed bras with four cups support the udder, leading to a marked increase in the milk yield.

The quickest wedding ceremony of all time took place in Detroit in 1978. Julie Filipetto married Gordon East in a ceremony that lasted just 15 seconds from start to finish. Maybe it had something to do with the fact that both bride and groom were in a zoo cage along with six fully grown lions . . .

A kangaroo in New South Wales jumped a record 42 feet in a single leap in 1968!

Chapter Eleven

IN THE DOGHOUSE

Pigs might fly, but they certainly can't drive! Jamie Eastwood, a farm worker from Elmsham in South Humberside made the mistake of leaving a pig in charge of his JCB when he got out to do some work. The pig, who had been riding with Jamie in the cab of the JCB, had obviously been paying close attention. As soon as Jamie was gone, he climbed into the driving seat and nudged the gear lever with his snout. The JCB lurched forward with the excited pig at the controls, knocking Jamie flat and pinning him down by his leg. After ten minutes of shouting for help, Jamie managed to attract the attention of a passer-by, who climbed into the cab, relegated the pig to the back seat and put the JCB into reverse.

It must have been a case of 'puppy love'. For weeks, obscene phone calls had made life a misery for a certain woman in the East Midlands. Whoever it was rang her again and again, making disgusting panting and slobbering noises down the phone at her at all hours of the day and night. Finally, she called in British Telecom experts to help her track down the pervert. They caught the culprit – a dog belonging to one of her closest friends, who had learned to press the automatic re-dial button on his owner's phone . . .

I've heard of the mouse that roared – but the mouse that ate a Mazda? Car-owner Don Howard certainly wishes he'd never heard of the ravenous rodent who wrecked his pride and joy. It all started when Don picked up his car from a local garage after leaving it in for repairs. He soon began to suspect he had a stowaway on board. There were telltale nibble marks in the packet of cough sweets he kept in the dashboard – and something had been shredded in the glove compartment. Then the mouse began to get seriously peckish. When Ron's car alarm started to go wrong, he checked in the boot – and found that a certain someone had chewed almost completely through a number of vital cables. Fearing that the car was now unsafe to drive, Ron had it towed to a nearby Mazda garage and put in an insurance claim. He was none too happy when the man from his insurance company fell about laughing and told him the story had made his week! Ron wasn't covered for 'Acts of Mouse', but his insurance company decided to honour his claim anyway and authorised a full search for the stowaway. The garage set to work stripping out seats, door panels, the dashboard and the entire steering column. After work costing hundreds of pounds, which left Ron's car little more than a shell, mechanics uncovered the mouse's home, snugly nestling on top of the heater box – but no mouse. With all the fuss and commotion, he'd probably decided to hitch a lift with some other unsuspecting driver . . .

It was certainly a Christmas to remember for Carmel and Peter Sandham – and for Sandy, their Labrador. As the family settled down to sleep on Christmas Eve at their home in Chadderton, Greater Manchester, Sandy decided that she simply couldn't wait until tomorrow for Christmas dinner. Following her nose, she trotted into the kitchen and proceeded to scoff a 17lb turkey, 2lbs of sausages, 2lbs of prawns, a plate of smoked salmon, 10 rashers of bacon, a pot of apple sauce, all the Paxo and a vast helping of potatoes, carrots, turnips and parsnips. Christmas dinner finished, Sandy's mind immediately turned to dessert. She decided to have 12 ginger and brandy puddings in lemon sauce, a tub of cream and a box of chocolates – just to round things off.

On Christmas morning, Carmel came downstairs to find an extremely bloated Sandy sprawled in the living room looking very pleased with herself and not a scrap of Christmas dinner left. 'I was frantic,' says Carmel. 'But with all the shops closed there was nothing I could do.' The family had to make do with what was left in the fridge – meat pie and chips and no dessert. They couldn't even enjoy the chocolate-filled advent calendar they'd bought. Sandy had eaten that two weeks earlier!

Castrol have developed a special suntan oil – especially for pigs. It seems that pigs raised outdoors are just as vulnerable to sunburn as the most fair-skinned of us

Chocoholic Spike the bull terrier pup must have thought he'd gone to heaven when he escaped from his owner's home in Bridgend, Mid-Glamorgan. The eleven-month-old's keen nose led him straight to the local Kwik-Save supermarket half a mile away – and shelves of tasty chocolate biscuits! Not realising that you actually have to pay for these things, Spike took a full-blooded leap straight into the pile of biscuits, scattering them in all directions and then started to eat as many as he could as quickly as he could. Supermarket staff rushed to the aisle where Spike was laying waste to their biscuit section and took prompt action. Manager Mark Trowbridge threw him out of the store three times, but each time Spike doubled back and launched himself at the biscuit shelves again. Finally, the staff used clattering shopping trolleys to drive the hungry hound into a storeroom. There they left him while the police were called – forgetting that the storeroom was stacked floor to ceiling with chocolate Easter eggs! There was only one thing for it, Spike must have reasoned. He'd have to eat his way to freedom! The pup piled into the chocolate eggs with gusto and had devoured most of them by the time his master, John Smithson arrived to collect him.

'Spike loves chocolate more than anything else,' sighed a resigned Mr Smithson. 'He can smell it a mile away!'

Pet parrots all over the UK are starting to dictate what their owners watch on television. The birds can hear the ultrasonic bleeps emitted by the TV controls when we change channels – and can mimic them well enough to fool the TV set!

It had to come – cat computer hackers! A Siamese cat called Missy recently strolled across her owner's computer keyboard at her home in Los Angeles – and accidentally hacked into a bank. By coincidence, the cat tapped out a special five-letter code sequence and erased $50,000 worth of customer account files. The bank later promised to upgrade its security.

It was asking for trouble – leaving two dogs in charge of a Range *Rover*. When Richard Fawcett parked his car in the centre of Newcastle upon Tyne last summer, he left it in first gear and forgot to put the handbrake on. No sooner had he and his family disappeared around the corner than his two boisterous collie dogs, Jess and Megan decided to climb into the driving seat. One of them managed to knock the gearstick into neutral and the Range Rover started rolling downhill, quickly gathering momentum. Startled passers-by watched as the car rolled past with two apparently grinning dogs peering over the dashboard. 'I thought I was seeing things,' said photographer Owen Humphries as the car passed him. 'I mean there were *collies* at the wheel . . .' Jess and Megan's joyride came to an abrupt end when they slammed into a parked BMW and came to rest against a parking meter.

Meanwhile, Mr Fawcett had come out to check on his dogs and had found his car missing. At first he thought it had been stolen, then looked down the road to see his car at the foot of the hill, surrounded by people. 'When I got down to my car, Jess and Megan were still inside,' he said later. 'They were furiously wagging their tails – loving all the attention they'd got for themselves.'

Back in the past, the quaint Cornish fishing village of Mousehole was a smugglers' paradise. Whisky, rum, perfumes and all kinds of contraband would pass along its narrow winding alleys at night. Today, there's still a lot of smuggling going on – but the contraband is now cat toys, balls of wool and teddy bears!

The criminal mastermind behind it all is a two-year-old tabby called Alfie. By night, he roams the back alleys of Mousehole, sneaks into homes through the cat flaps while the occupants are asleep – and makes off with whatever takes his fancy. Usually, he smuggles out other cats' toys, but he's also been known to return home with balls of wool, strings of beads, socks, scarves, bin bags, baseball caps and even a teddy significantly larger than himself!

No one is safe. Neighbours Graham and Jill Prodger fitted a magnetic cat flap so only their two cats, Minnie and Bugs, could get in. Undeterred, Alfie cased the joint and found the flaw in the Prodgers' security system. He has worked out that, by sticking his claws into the rubber seal, he can get one paw inside and then wedge the cat flap open.

'Alfie was a juvenile delinquent,' his owner, Pat Smith, admits resignedly. 'It started when he was just a few months old. I've had cats all my life – but never a thieving cat. He's a wicked boy. He's got a brother called Bertie. Bertie is a good boy.'

Homing pigeons are amazing creatures but boy, when they miss, they can miss by a mile – or 6,000 miles in the case of Percy. Percy the racing pigeon set off from Folkestone in Kent in 1992, aiming for home in Billingham, Cleveland. Instead, he ended up in Shanghai, China, 6,000 miles off course!

Percy's owner, George Gamble, had given him up for lost. Five years had passed when in March 1997 George was stunned to get a phone call from a Chinese woman who had identified Percy through the code attached to his leg. He was alive and well and – probably – too ashamed to come home.

However, when the full story came out, it looked as if Percy hadn't let his profession down after all. Blown off course over the North Sea on his way home, the bird had taken refuge on an oil rig. Here he was adopted by a Chinese crew member on an oil tanker who decided to take him home for a pigeon-fancying friend. Shanghaied, Percy found himself on the proverbial 'slow boat to China', sailing via Rotterdam, the Bay of Biscay, the Mediterranean, then the Suez Canal, and right across the Indian Ocean to China. Once there, Percy didn't have a clue how to get home and settled down to the new world of Chinese homing pigeon racing, where he proved himself a star.

Percy isn't the first racing pigeon to go East. When pigeon fancier Phil Hoddinott let his pigeon go on its maiden flight from Sussex to Dorset in 1992, it went missing for four years, before he got a phone call from Manchuria saying it had turned up there!

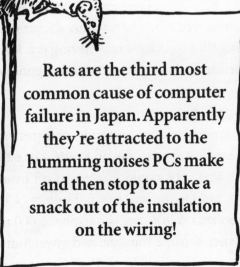

Rats are the third most common cause of computer failure in Japan. Apparently they're attracted to the humming noises PCs make and then stop to make a snack out of the insulation on the wiring!

Sedgewick the cat lived in Cambridgeshire and one cold night he sought warmth in a local electricity sub-station. The warmth he got, though, was more than he bargained for. In the darkness Sedgewick brushed up against a switch that controlled over 30,000 volts. This not only cut off the electricity to 40,000 Cambridge homes, it also left Sedgewick a bit frazzled. He reached home looking like, well, something the cat had dragged in, but made a miraculous recovery after his electrifying experience.

You may have heard the expression 'as drunk as a skunk' but how about 'as tanked up as an elephant'? It happened in Tanzania when a herd of elephants went on the rampage after eating fermented fruit. Rangers in their game park saw them running aimlessly around, uprooting trees and small bushes and knocking into one another until at last they fell asleep. Whether they woke the next day with a jumbo-sized hangover is unknown.

Coco the African Grey Parrot had a very special talent – driving the German shepherd he lived with absolutely crazy. Heiko the German shepherd was exceptionally well trained – and that was the problem. Coco had learned to mimic his master's voice and was for ever giving Heiko orders which the poor dog felt compelled to obey. 'Heel!' the parrot would screech, 'Stay! Sit! Come! Roll over! Play dead! Bad girl! Good girl!' Poor Heiko didn't know if she was coming or going!

Queen Elizabeth the Queen Mother celebrated her 90th birthday in 1990 with a march-by at Horse Guards Parade, London. Alongside such prestigious regiments as the Household Cavalry and the Dragoon Guards was to march an Aberdeen Angus bull, dressed in its finery.

The procession called for the bull to march at 116 paces to the minute in order to keep up with the soldiers accompanying it. However, in rehearsal, it couldn't manage this, not even the 90 paces per minute expected of the ninety-year-old Chelsea Pensioners, also in the parade.

On the day, despite these setbacks, the bull *did* parade in front of the Queen Mother, although not as planned – it was driven past her on a trailer.

Guinness has been prescribed for horses suffering from colic

Goats are renowned for eating anything – and one goat in Los Angeles not only demonstrated his love of ice-cream, he also stole the van it came in.

It happened when the driver had parked to make a delivery. Without warning, the goat jumped through the open doorway into the cab and accidentally released the handbrake.

The ice-cream van careered down a hill before crashing into a tree, scattering ice-cream everywhere. The goat jumped from the cab, helped himself to a minty choc ice then trotted off, none the worse for his ordeal.

Rocky the St Bernard is one of the only dogs to have done 'bird'. He was arrested for shoplifting in 1991 and spent five days in an animal shelter for his crime. It happened in the Gloucester township in New Jersey. It was a freezing cold day, he needed to warm up – and the local supermarket looked inviting.

After figuring out how the automatic doors worked, Rocky casually entered the shop and sauntered down the aisles, to the amazement of the other shoppers and staff.

At last Rocky found something he really wanted – a huge bag of treats from the pet food section. He took the bag in his mouth and nonchalantly walked out.

Now Rocky was a big dog, and no one wanted to try and stop him so the police were called. When they arrived at the scene, Rocky was definitely not going to give up his pet treats, and kept running off when they approached.

When at last he was caught Rocky was charged with resisting arrest and for handling (or in his case, pawing) stolen goods.

After serving his time at the animal shelter he was reunited with his owner – hopefully having learned his lesson!

Congo the chimp loved a tipple or two – or three, or four – and when his owner, Mario Cervantes went out, leaving one in their New York apartment, Congo raided the drinks cabinet. After downing three bottles of beer and a half-bottle of vodka, the alcoholic ape got out of the window and climbed down into the street below, where he proceeded to break windows, be generally obnoxious, and bite a neighbour.

He finally returned home after Mario pleaded with him in the middle of the street. Reports say he's now off the drink – and on the wagon!

John Wilson was really proud of a trick he taught his
Alsatian – sliding a bolt across to lock his shed door. He
wasn't so proud, though, when his over-eager dog slid the bolt
home while John was inside: he had to spend the night there
before he could be released.

In the eighteenth century,
the 2nd Earl of Montague
built an OAPs' home for
cows and horses (or
should we say an old
animals' home?)

Police stopped motorcyclist Roger Bullen while he was
riding in Chingford, Essex. It wasn't because he was
speeding, or riding without a crash helmet – it was because his
tomcat Maurice was riding pillion.

According to Roger, Maurice loved to go out on the bike, a
Honda 250. They had made numerous trips to the shops or just
to go sightseeing, and Maurice only got upset if Roger went over
30mph. At this speed he must have felt he was in danger of
falling off, and always signalled his concern by digging his claws
into Roger's back.

In 1987 an elephant called Frederick had to be rescued by
crane when he fell into a lake in a Danish wildlife park.
The reason for his tumble was like a scene out of a Benny Hill
show – he was trying to escape from six amorous female
elephants who were chasing him round the zoo!

For a little chimp, Bimbo was pretty strong. When he arrived at the San Francisco Zoo in 1937 he needed five keepers to control him. However, it was soon evident that he was just mischievous rather than violent. Bimbo demonstrated acute intelligence, which, combined with cunning and a delicious sense of humour caused absolute havoc in the 34 years he spent at the zoo.

He loved food, and on many occasions he would break into other chimps' compounds to steal theirs, ripping off the locks from the separating doors and sneaking in. His natural sense of rhythm captivated visitors, who would watch for hours as he gyrated and skipped across his cage. He particularly liked to trip the light fantastic during rainstorms, and his 'rain dance' became a star attraction. Mind you, onlookers had to be careful! One of Bimbo's other skills was far less 'spectator friendly'. He would fill his mouth with water and unerringly squirt any visitor he didn't like the look of!

In 1987 Haringey Council voted to open a £56,000 hostel-cum-hotel for stray cats as a bold blow against 'rampant anti-cat discrimination in the community'

Early live BBC wildlife programmes often ended in complete chaos. On one occasion, a giant fruit bat which was being featured in a show, took off and swooped up to the high studio ceiling, attracted by heat rising from the lights.

Attempts to entice it down failed and for weeks afterwards the beast made 'unscheduled appearances' on all sorts of TV shows, causing the actors to run shrieking for cover! Delighted viewers were also treated to the sight of news readers being 'dive-bombed' by the fruit bat as they struggled to read the headlines!

Chester Zoo couldn't understand what was wrong with their telephone system. For six months in 1964 it would work sometimes, and then not at other times. Telephone engineers were baffled, and thoroughly fed up with being called out. They could find absolutely nothing wrong. It was zoo staff who cracked it. George the giraffe had taken a liking to the telephone wires strung above his enclosure and would lick them whenever the mood took him. The wires tasted deliciously salty – and their 50 volt charge must have given him an intoxicating tingle! He was reportedly quite upset when the telephone engineers raised the wires another three feet so they were out of his reach . . .

Elephant bandits are holding drivers to ransom on the road through the Garampani wildlife sanctuary in north-east India. They block the road in front of trucks and cars and refuse to budge until they receive a payment of fruit or sugar cane. Those who refuse to pay up risk having their vehicles barged off the road.

While Jimmy Carter was President he often took a fishing break in his home state of Georgia. However, even when 'off duty' he was always under surveillance by the White House security forces. On one particular trip, agents were in the woods surrounding the lake, on the shore and even in nearby dinghies. But for all their security measures, they failed to stop one crazed attacker from reaching the President. A vicious wild rabbit streaked across the lake, climbed into Carter's boat and tried to bite him. The brave President fought off his attacker with an oar and the Western world was safe once more.

His owners wanted to take him to the vet, but Blacky the tomcat had other ideas. He fled from his house – and straight into the nearest supermarket in his home town of Thun, in Switzerland. Once inside, he made for the choice meats and sausages department where he managed to hole up for several days before staff winkled him out.

Cocky, an Australian white cockatoo who belonged to an Adelaide innkeeper in the early 1900s, was infamous for shouting obscenities at unsuspecting guests and he could soon pick up any voice and imitate it to perfection!

One of his meanest tricks was to imitate the calls of wagon drivers who'd stopped at the inn for refreshment. Cocky's calls were so accurate that he'd often cause the wagon team to set off, leaving their drivers behind. His best impersonation, however, was of a fierce dogfight. He could keep this going for so long that men would rush into the bar, expecting to have to separate two giant howling animals. All they ever found was little Cocky, perched on the bar in mid-performance.

Chapter Twelve
ANIMAL CRACKERS

Most cats bring in mice or birds. Maurice the cat, however, likes to do things a little differently. He brings home women's underwear. So far, he has presented his mistress with over 60 different bras, vests and knickers as proof of his hunting prowess. His mistress, Fiona, who lives in Wellington, New Zealand, has dutifully washed, ironed and folded every single item, but so far no one has come forward to claim them.

Another master cat burglar is the aptly named Attila, from Chard in Somerset. He breaks into neighbours' houses – through their cat flaps, naturally – and steals the biggest cuddly toy he can find. According to his owner, Wendy Singleton, Attila has brought home at least 12 cuddly toys including a foot-high pink elephant! 'He must have really had to struggle to get that through the cat flap,' Wendy says.

It's true that an elephant never forgets. At least that's what one German family discovered while they were staying at a camp site in the Masai Mara in Africa. The creature in question was a semi-tame bull elephant who used to wander out of the bush at meal times, and be fed bread rolls by the guests.

One day, the elephant came into the clearing as usual, but instead of stopping for the rolls he carefully wove his way in between tables and chairs until he reached a German family that had just arrived. He stopped in front of them and angrily knocked over their table with his trunk before disappearing back into the bush. The camp staff had never seen anything like it and were very apologetic to their new guests. The next night, the same German family were again settling down for a meal at the same table, when the elephant appeared out of the bush once more. Again, he immediately made his way over to the family, and with a huge trumpet, pushed over the table once more.

The family weren't going to take any chances on the third night so they changed tables and moved well away. As expected, the elephant arrived and made his way straight to the original table, and stopped. The German family had gone. He looked all around the terrace until he finally spotted them, then walked over to their new table and proceeded to knock it to bits. Not surprisingly the family weren't going to take any more chances: they ran to their tent, whereupon the elephant ripped heavy branches off the nearby trees and barricaded them inside.

No one has the slightest idea what might have brought about this behaviour, but you can guess what the elephant's new nickname is. Yes . . . Churchill, of course!

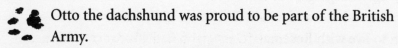 Otto the dachshund was proud to be part of the British Army.

His master was an English brigadier in command of a Gurkha regiment in northern India, and every day he'd accompany him on morning inspection on the parade ground. In fact, he was so enthusiastic that he would usually arrive early, giving the Gurkhas a warning that the Brigadier was on his way. The soldiers would then stand swiftly to attention, ready for their commanding officer's arrival.

One morning, the Brigadier fell sick, so Otto set off without him. Seeing him coming, every soldier on the base quickly scrambled on to the parade ground and stood to attention. The little dog trotted in and out of the ranks, proudly inspecting them, then wandered off home again – leaving the entire highly disciplined regiment standing in the baking sun for hours with no one to dismiss them . . .

Fudge the boxer dog made the mistake of swallowing a novelty musical watch. For several weeks he chimed the notes of Glen Miller's 'American Patrol' at 6.45a.m. and 6.45p.m. precisely!

We all realise that children can suffer greatly when their parents get divorced, but how much thought do we give to the pets? William, an amazon blue parrot had to go through an agonising fight for custody of him when his owners divorced. In the end, it was decided to rehouse him completely. He went on to live with Rosemary Dean, who had a heart condition and had thought that the parrot would help to calm her down. Not a bit of it! William keeps reliving the fierce quarrels his previous owners had before their divorce – playing both sides of the argument. He screeches out their angry words to each other, and even mimics the wife's crying. Just to add insult to injury, he can also do an uncanny impersonation of the couple's yappy little terrier – so Rosemary's household is in constant uproar.

Neighbours have even made complaints about her to their housing authority, saying that they can hear her rowing with a man all the time.

Despite it all, Rosemary is determined that William won't get thrown out again. 'I'm not parting with him. I love him and he really makes me laugh,' she says.

Orangutans sometimes talk to each other by burping!

Forget greyhounds – if you really want to see some fast paced racing action, then you need to go to the All-Alaskan Racing Pigs finals! Eight championship porkers compete in knockout rounds for the title of the fastest thing on four trotters. There's even an All-Alaskan Racing Pigs club, whose motto is 'Come rain or swine, the sow must go on'!

In 1936, some bright young entrepreneur opened the world's first cat racetrack at Portisham in Dorset, complete with electric mice for the cats to chase. The public's enthusiasm for the idea was considerable, much more so than the cats who were supposed to take part. Most were perfectly happy to stay curled up asleep in their starting traps; or they preferred tussling with other competitors to chasing an electric mouse. The idea was soon abandoned.

The passengers on board the Philippines Airlines flight from Manila to Tokyo were dozing or watching the in-flight movie when a loud scream went up from the back of the aircraft. Fearing a hijacker, everyone turned round and a stewardess rushed to see what the commotion was.

By now, several passengers were frozen in fear as they stared up at an overhead luggage locker that was slightly open. Poking its head out and looking rather inquisitively at the terrified passengers was a large snake. Jumping into action, the cabin crew managed to get it safely back into the locker and keep it there until the aircraft landed in Japan.

Since no one claimed the snake, airline officials assume it was a slippery stowaway that had climbed aboard while the aircraft was being cleaned and serviced in Manila.

It's not unusual for an airline to be sued – but it is if the action is taken by a dog! Ari, a mongrel, was travelling on a US Air flight in a pet carrier but got separated from his owner, a lawyer, after flying from Tampa, Florida to Washington, DC. It seemed that the lawyer was looking for his luggage on one carousel – while Ari circled helplessly on another. The lawyer, acting for Ari, sued US Air for $50,000 compensation for distress and hardship. The case, however, was thrown out – the judge ruled that dogs were not American citizens, and therefore could not sue the airline.

For years, Twig the Shetland collie had been drinking out of the same old blue and white dish. One day, his owner, Mrs Lesley Joseph, took him along with her to the village hall to see an antiques show. She brought the little dish along, in case Twig got thirsty and needed a drink. An astonished Sotheby's expert snatched it up off the floor and away from Twig, telling Mrs Joseph that it was in fact a rare Chinese vase. It subsequently sold at auction for £6,200.

I've heard of mutton dressed as lamb – but never lambs dressed as foxes! However, that's the new wheeze Jim Watts has come up with on his farm in Calne, Wiltshire. Worried about attacks on the newborns in his flock, Jim has taken to dressing the young 'uns up in bright orange jackets! From a distance they look like foxes themselves, and any fox, being a solitary creature by nature, prefers to give them a clear berth.

Some of Jim's neighbours have complained that bright orange sheep spoil the look of the countryside, but he's unrepentant. 'As long as my lambs are happy, I don't care!' he says.

The most unusual cat lover in the world is probably a gorilla called Koko. Koko, who can 'talk' to staff at her home in the Gorilla Foundation in California using sign language, first saw cats when her trainer, Dr Penny Patterson of Stanford University, showed her picture books of *Puss in Boots* and the *Three Little Kittens*. As her skill is using sign language progressed, Dr Patterson noticed that Koko kept pulling two fingers across her cheeks to represent a cat – Koko wanted her own pet!

In 1984 Koko was introduced to an abandoned male kitten. She immediately took to him, signing 'love that' and named him (also by signing) 'All Ball'. All Ball was more than a pet – she was Koko's surrogate child and was treated like that. Both gorilla and kitten would play for hours together; Koko summed up how she felt about her new baby by signing 'soft good cat'. Sadly, All Ball died after being run over and Koko was heartbroken. The staff gave her a tiny ginger Manx kitten as a replacement. Koko named it herself. She called the kitten 'Lips-Lipstick' and took to gently hugging it in her arms. 'My cat good!' she told staff proudly in her sign language.

Thoroughbred racehorse Remittance Man has two claims to fame. He won the prestigious Queen Mother Chase at Cheltenham in 1992 – and he's the only racehorse to own a pet sheep. His owners noticed that Remittance Man was lonely, because he wasn't allowed to play with other horses at the stables in case he had an accident. So, they decided to get him a pet sheep of his own for company. Remittance Man has had three woolly companions during his career. They all travelled with him to racing events to keep him company, and he now lives in glorious retirement in Oxfordshire together with his latest friend, the sheep called Nobby.

In 1988 a herd of Friesian cows on a Cornish farm were suffering from sore feet since they spent nearly six months of the year on the farm's concrete flooring. They were so upset that they stopped producing milk. The farmer had to come up with a solution – and quickly. He went down to his local shoe shop and ordered each cow two extra-comfortable pairs of green wellington boots!

Tyras was a black Great Dane who was the constant companion and bodyguard of Prince Otto von Bismarck of Germany. On one famous occasion, Bismarck was engrossed in some delicate diplomatic negotiations with the Russian Foreign Minister. The Russian was very demonstrative and was waving his arms about just as Tyras walked into the room. The dog assumed that Bismarck was being attacked and leapt at the 'assailant', knocking him to the floor. Fortunately, the Russian Minister accepted Bismarck's profuse apologies. Wars have started over less.

Mutley the mongrel is a real daredevil dog. He belongs to Gene Alba in the US and joins in all Gene's leisure pursuits. Mutley goes skiing with him and even accompanies him scuba diving, wearing a custom-made miniature diving suit. To get about he rides pillion on Gene's motorcycle, wearing a specially adapted canine crash helmet.

The travelling arrangements of an English retriever named Sally were a lot more sedate. She was a familiar sight in Egham, Surrey in the 1950s, majestically sitting up in a wicker basket attached to the front of an 1898 motorcycle belonging to her owner, Mr Williamson.

The ancient Egyptians worshipped cats, but more recently two felines have displayed a significant interest in religion. The first was a small Burmese cat named Honey who was one of the regular congregation at a small Lincolnshire church. She sat to attention during sermons (one of the few parishioners that did) and mewed along with the organ music, accompanying the church choir.

A similar thing happened on the other side of the world at a Buddhist temple in Malaysia. In 1988 a stray cat walked in and joined the monks who were deep in meditation. It's reported that the cat sat up on his hind legs and assumed the nearest it could get to the lotus position. After that it came back each day for meditation sessions, and some monks believe it's the reincarnation of Buddha himself!

Mincha is probably the most single-minded cat I've ever come across – and that's saying something! She lived in Buenos Aires in Argentina and one day ran up a 40-foot-high tree – never to come down again. She lived in the branches, on food passed up to her on a pole by the locals. A milkman even delivered a daily pinta. Mincha's remote location didn't prevent her from receiving admirers, however – six years after disappearing up the tree she gave birth to kittens.

Perhaps it's not surprising. A local newspaper once ran a sad little notice saying that a kitten had gone missing in the area. It was described as 'black and white and answering to the name "Go Away"...'

In Japan recently, police were called to a village to catch and arrest a fiend who was stealing women's underwear from washing lines. A stake-out was set up and in time the thieves were caught – a team of wild monkeys. It seemed that the pestilential primates raided the village for food, but took the lingerie for kicks!

In 1982 the authorities warned travellers to the hills of Omei in central China to be on their guard against a gang of three 'monkey muggers'. The monkeys attacked walkers and 60 separate incidents had been reported over a six-month period. Visitors to the region were advised to carry extra food to throw at their attackers. This would distract them long enough for the walkers to make their escape.

In 1865 Mark Twain wrote a story, 'The Celebrated Jumping Frogs of Calaveras County, California' about a local competition which took place to find the frog who could jump the furthest.

This tradition still carries on today at Angels Camp in California, about 120 miles east of San Francisco. It's now known as the Calaveras County Jumping Frog Jubilee and the two-day event attracts 40,000 entrants from all over the USA. The all-time record was held for years by a swamp frog called Corrision who jumped 18 feet and half an inch in May 1970. However, in May 1980 this was shattered by a Salinas frog called Oh-No, who leapt into the record books with an amazing 19 feet, nine and a half inches, beating 1,900 other froggie competitors.

The rules are simple. Each frog makes three consecutive jumps, in as straight a line as possible – with the total distance counting.

In February 1980 a stray cat was trapped in a Bradford alley by a dog. The only way out was upwards. The cat leapt up the sheer brick wall and climbed, and climbed . . . and climbed – until she found herself 70 feet up a tower block, cowering in a recess just below the roof. She was rescued by the RSPCA, who determined that she'd used the pebbledashed exterior of the flats for grip.

Once safely reunited with the ground the stray was given an apt name – Bonington, after the British mountaineer.

When Maria Smith's budgie suddenly came out with a string of numbers she took the hint – and used them to win £10 on the National Lottery. Now, she says, Peter the budgie repeats these numbers religiously, along with his home phone number and occasionally the odd swear word!

Ravens have made their home on the battlements of the Tower of London since it was built in 1066 and legend has it that if they leave, 'the Tower will fall and the glory of Britain will vanish' (the ravens' wings are clipped to prevent this happening). Today, the ravens (and the Tower) are guarded by Yeomen Warders who wear uniforms based on those of the bodyguards who protected King Henry VII.

The first talking budgie belonged to a convict, Thomas Watling, who was sent to the penal colony of New South Wales in 1788 for counterfeiting banknotes. Life for Thomas wasn't that bad; he soon became assistant to the chief physician, Dr James White.

This position gave him lots of time to study the Australian wildlife and he soon became interested in the brightly coloured budgerigars – birds that he'd never seen before. It wasn't long before he'd tamed one and spent hours of his spare time coaxing it to talk.

One day Dr White was looking for Watling. He wasn't in his room and the doctor was just about to leave when a shrill voice said, 'How'd you do, Dr White.'

The doctor was astounded to discover that it was a bird talking – the first budgie on record to do so.

Watling was eventually pardoned but decided to stay in New South Wales. He continued studying and training budgies until the day he died.

When you think of birds found in the desert you usually think of vultures – not pelicans. But, if you find yourself travelling through the deserts of the south-western United States, you may well come across a stranded pelican looking all forlorn at the side of the road. It happens more often than you might think.

They get blown way off course by monsoon winds off the Pacific Coast and are then dumped exhausted and lost in the desert. Fortunately, help is at hand in the form of the airline American West. They've instituted a special programme to fly pelicans back to a Californian wildlife sanctuary where they can return to the water. That must make American West the pelicans' favourite airline . . .

In California a dog called Jenny had a tree climbing permit. It was issued by San Francisco's Parks and Recreations Department in recognition of Jenny's unusual ability to climb 45 feet up a tree

Mrs Debra Degan was out on her farm in Brisbane, Australia on 7 January 1989 when she heard the sound of thunder. She expected a late summer storm to approach – which it did. The only thing was that it rained sardines! It's thought that a strong wind had whipped the sardines from the sea and carried them into the air, then 30 miles inland, where they fell to the earth as rain.

The oldest authenticated dog that ever lived was Adjutant, a black Labrador that lived with his owner on a Lincolnshire estate. He was born in August 1936 and died in November 1963, which means he reached the grand old age of twenty-seven, the doggie equivalent of 189 of our years.

In 1984 council workers in Paris were shocked as they made one of their regular inspections of the ancient sewer system. Wandering through the dark, damp tunnels was a crocodile. It was about three feet in length and was thought to be four years old. The most likely theory is that the croc was flushed down the toilet when it was a lot younger, and had adapted to living in the sewers. The council called in the fire brigade, who were more used to rescuing cats from trees than crocodiles from pipes. They managed to overpower it and transported it to the Jardin des Plantes in Paris where its habitat was a pleasant vivarium.

On the other hand, crocodiles living in sewers are no surprise to residents of Manzini, in Swaziland, where they're put in for two reasons. Firstly, they're a cheap and effective way of getting rid of waste. Secondly, and more importantly, every croc in the sewers is one less in the rivers – so locals can cross those rivers in much greater safety.

The original Roland Rat was the sole companion of Alberto Pagini, an Italian criminal charged with fraud. Alone in his cell in Rome's Regina Coeli prison, Alberto befriended the rat (whom he named Roland), and played with him, feeding him scraps from his own meals. Roland took Alberto's mind off his long prison sentence, and on the day of his release, Alberto took him to a nearby bar to celebrate.

Unfortunately, this bar had been plagued by rats and the manager mistook Roland for one of them, lashing out at him with an old bottle and hitting him on the head.

Alberto was shocked and horrified by this – and he sued the manager for killing his pet. It's not recorded what happened in court, but Roland was stuffed and kept by Alberto as a constant reminder of his loyal companionship.

Motorcyclist Pete Robinson of Penarth, South Wales has a pillion passenger with a difference. It's his six-year-old pet iguana, Stumpy. What's more, the four-foot-long lizard has his own miniature leather jacket complete with pockets and a chrome zip. At first, the pet shop that supplied the clothes for Stumpy thought that Pete was joking when he asked them for biker gear for his pet. However they soon managed to track down a jacket at a shop in California. Pete said, 'You should have seen Stumpy's face when the jacket arrived. He was delighted.'

As Pete zooms along on his Kawasaki 250, Stumpy rides with him, clinging to Pete's back or shoulder. Pete isn't reckless and always has the welfare of his pet in mind. He's even thinking of buying Stumpy an iguana-size crash helmet. As Pete says, 'Well, he needs to be safe.'

'I really don't think I could consent to go to heaven if I thought that there would be no animals there'
GEORGE BERNARD SHAW